Global Integrated Intelligence, Surveillance, & Reconnaissance Operations

Air Force Doctrine Document 2-0

6 January 2012

This document complements related discussion found in Joint Publication 2-0,
Joint Intelligence

BY ORDER OF THE
SECRETARY OF THE AIR FORCE

AIR FORCE DOCTRINE DOCUMENT 2-0
6 JANUARY 2012

SUMMARY OF CHANGES

This document is substantially revised and must be completely reviewed. The structure of the document has been changed to present information in a more cohesive manner. The concept of *"Global Integrated"* Intelligence, Surveillance and Reconnaissance (ISR) operations is introduced and defined versus historical ISR operations (Chapter 1). A discussion of the Air Force Distributed Common Ground System has been added (Chapter 2). The ISR process of Planning and Direction, Collection, Processing and Exploitation, Analysis and Production, and Dissemination (PCPAD) is detailed throughout.

Supersedes: AFDD 2-0, 17 July 2007
OPR: LeMay Center/DDS
Certified by: LeMay Center/CC (Maj Gen Thomas K. Andersen)
Pages: 78
Accessibility: Available on the e-publishing website at www.e-publishing.af.mil for downloading
Releasability: There are no releasability restrictions on this publication
Approved by: NORTON A. SCHWARTZ, General, USAF
                    Chief of Staff

FOREWORD

Intelligence, surveillance, and reconnaissance (ISR) from the air date back to the use of balloons to observe the adversary during the French Revolution. In today's knowledge-based environment, we observe and analyze the meaning and impact of a wide variety of events and convey useful, timely intelligence on our adversaries' capabilities and intentions to decision-makers. However, in this "Age of Information," we've expanded our ISR capabilities to operate from and through air, space, and cyberspace to achieve desired effects across the range of military operations in contested and denied environments in support of US national security objectives.

The Air Force ISR enterprise assures Air Force Global Vigilance, Reach, and Power and provides desired effects to combatant commanders. We disseminate knowledge to better support decision-makers and shape operations. Still, we must never lose sight of the need for continuing to evaluate our methodologies for employing and integrating ISR capabilities vice simply increasing the density of ISR capabilities.

The Air Force completed a four year ISR transformation addressing ISR organization, personnel, and capabilities to more efficiently support all MAJCOMs and optimize force presentation to Combat Air Forces. Our Total Force ISR capabilities integrated and synchronized with National and Defense ISR; and with Army, Navy, Marine, Allied, and coalition ISR capabilities provide the US a clear advantage over our adversaries.

AF ISR has been engaged in wartime and peacetime operations for decades and has responded by demonstrating and projecting US power globally. We have come a long way from the days of wondering what is going on just over the next hill, or half a world away. As we have learned in the current conflicts, Air Force ISR is operations and shapes and drives decision-making. The Office of the Secretary of Defense, as well as the Joint Staff, does not segregate Intelligence, Surveillance, and Reconnaissance; nor will we. ISR is often the first capability a combatant commander requests and employs prior to and upon the initiation of military operations. Often it must persist even after major combat operations have ended. Through global integrated ISR, the Air Force will continue to protect America and her interests.

NORTON A. SCHWARTZ
General, USAF
Chief of Staff

TABLE OF CONTENTS

PREFACE

Air Force Doctrine Document (AFDD) 2-0, Global Integrated Intelligence, Surveillance, and Reconnaissance (ISR) Operations, is the Air Force's keystone doctrinal publication on global integrated ISR and defines how the Service plans and conducts these operations to enable Joint Operations. It compiles the best practices of how an Airman conducts and employs ISR capabilities and why global integrated ISR is unique. The three chapters define global integrated ISR, the command relationships and authorities that enable it, and how these operations are planned and conducted.

Chapter One, *Fundamentals of Global Integrated ISR Operations*, describes global integrated ISR, answering "What is global integrated ISR?" and how it is implemented to support the Air Force and its missions. It focuses on: the definition of global integrated ISR; the Airman's perspective; global integrated ISR as a service core function (SCF); basic global integrated ISR principles; and policy and guidance for global integrated ISR operations. It also outlines how cross-domain integration and global integrated ISR are linked. Finally, it introduces the Air Force process of planning and direction, collection, processing and exploitation, analysis and production, and dissemination (PCPAD).

Chapter Two, *Command and Organization of Global Integrated ISR Forces*, discusses the command and organization of Air Force global integrated ISR forces. It discusses the roles of commanders in regards to the planning and execution of global integrated ISR operations. It outlines the roles and responsibilities of global integrated ISR linked personnel within and outside of the ISR Division of the Air Operations Center (AOC). It discusses global integrated ISR presentation of forces considerations and guidance to include remote and distributed operations. It provides an overview of the roles of global integrated ISR associated personnel within different Air Force echelons and mission sets. It details the special relationships required for specific missions and the roles in homeland and counterdrug operations, and irregular warfare considerations.

Chapter Three, *The Global Integrated ISR Process*, answers the question, "How does the Air Force perform global integrated ISR operations?" This section defines the various intelligence disciplines and their subsets. It discusses the different types of guidance to be considered when planning global integrated ISR operations. It outlines the multiple types of ISR resources that are available for employment. It outlines the Air Force global integrated ISR process of PCPAD. Finally, it describes the different methodologies that PCPAD supports and the types of global integrated ISR products created.

The principal audience for this publication is all Airmen, both uniformed and civilian. It is the defining document for ISR operations in the United States Air Force.

CHAPTER ONE

FUNDAMENTALS OF GLOBAL INTEGRATED INTELLIGENCE, SURVEILLANCE, AND RECONNAISSANCE OPERATIONS

Our ISR capabilities are key to operating in today's information dominated environment...getting the right information to the right people to make the best possible decisions. And ISR demands will only increase in future conflicts.

— **Lt Gen Larry D. James**
Deputy Chief of Staff for ISR

ISR DEFINED

JP 1-02, *Department of Defense (DOD) Dictionary of Military and Associated Terms* defines intelligence, surveillance, and reconnaissance (ISR) as: "An activity that synchronizes and integrates the planning and operations of sensors, assets, processing, exploitation, and dissemination systems **in direct support** of current and future operations. This is an integrated intelligence operations function." ISR consists of separate elements but requires treatment as an integrated whole in order to be optimized.

GLOBAL INTEGRATED ISR DEFINED

DOD Directive (DODD) 5100.01, *Functions of the Department of Defense and Its Major Components* directs the Air Force to "Provide timely, global integrated ISR capability and capacity from forward deployed locations and globally distributed centers to support world-wide operations." Global integrated ISR is defined as cross-domain synchronization and integration of the planning and operation of ISR assets; sensors; processing, exploitation and dissemination systems; and, analysis and production capabilities across the globe to enable current and future operations. This definition differs from the joint definition of ISR in that the Air Force eliminates references to "in direct support of...operations." In addition to providing direct support to operations, ISR operations are also conducted to inform strategy, planning, and assessment.

Global integrated ISR enables utilization of multiple assets from multiple geographic commands; collecting data across all domains that may satisfy strategic, operational and tactical requirements; which may be used by national, joint or service specific personnel or any combination thereof. Global integrated ISR enables the integration of this collected information to deliver intelligence to the right person at the right time, anywhere on the globe. Figure 1.1 depicts the global presence of the AF ISR Enterprise.

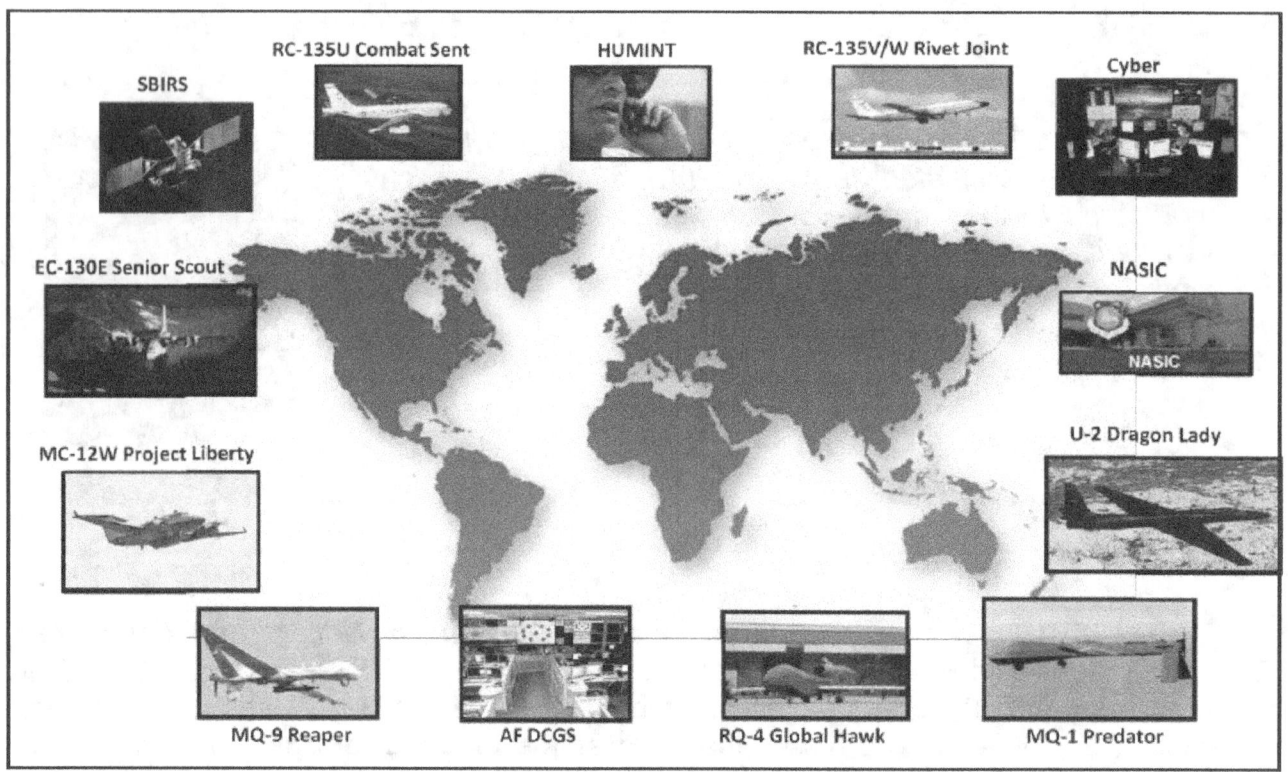

Figure 1.1. Global ISR Presence

An example of how the AF ISR enterprise projects global presence is through distributed operations. A global integrated Predator mission includes the aircraft, the datalinks that allow it to be flown remotely from a location outside of theater, and all of the networks that allow its data to be streamed in near real-time to many locations around the world. It also includes the analytic capability being leveraged outside of theater that allows global collaboration to exploit the collected data, plus the dissemination capability that allows finished intelligence to flow back to multiple end users and stored for future reference. This is the true difference between ISR operations and global integrated ISR operations.

The ultimate goal of global integrated ISR operations is to achieve desired effects in support of national security objectives through knowledge dominance of the operating environment and adversary intentions. JP 2-0, *Joint Intelligence*, states that "information is of greatest value when it contributes to or shapes the commander's decision-making by providing reasoned insight into future conditions or situations."[1]

---

[1] JP 2-0, *Joint Intelligence*

Global integrated ISR operations provide actionable intelligence to the commander in the fastest way possible.

AIRMAN'S PERSPECTIVE ON GLOBAL INTEGRATED ISR

First and foremost, global integrated ISR operations are domain, service and platform neutral. The focus is on meeting information requirements and providing actionable intelligence to commanders. Global integrated ISR is a key enabler and a force multiplier when integrated with the other service core functions (SCFs). It is further enhanced when integrated with joint, defense, national, and coalition ISR. Global integrated ISR is the linchpin of effects based operations and enables integration and synchronization of assets, people, processes, and information across all domains, to inform the commander's decision cycle.

ISR is indivisible. The evolution of technology, information, and service culture enabled a move from the segregation of operations and intelligence to integration of operations and intelligence. The elements of ISR are interdependent and mutually supporting to compress the Find, Fix, Track, Target, Engage, and Assess process from days to minutes. Figure 1.2 depicts the information in war revolution and the integration of operations and intelligence.

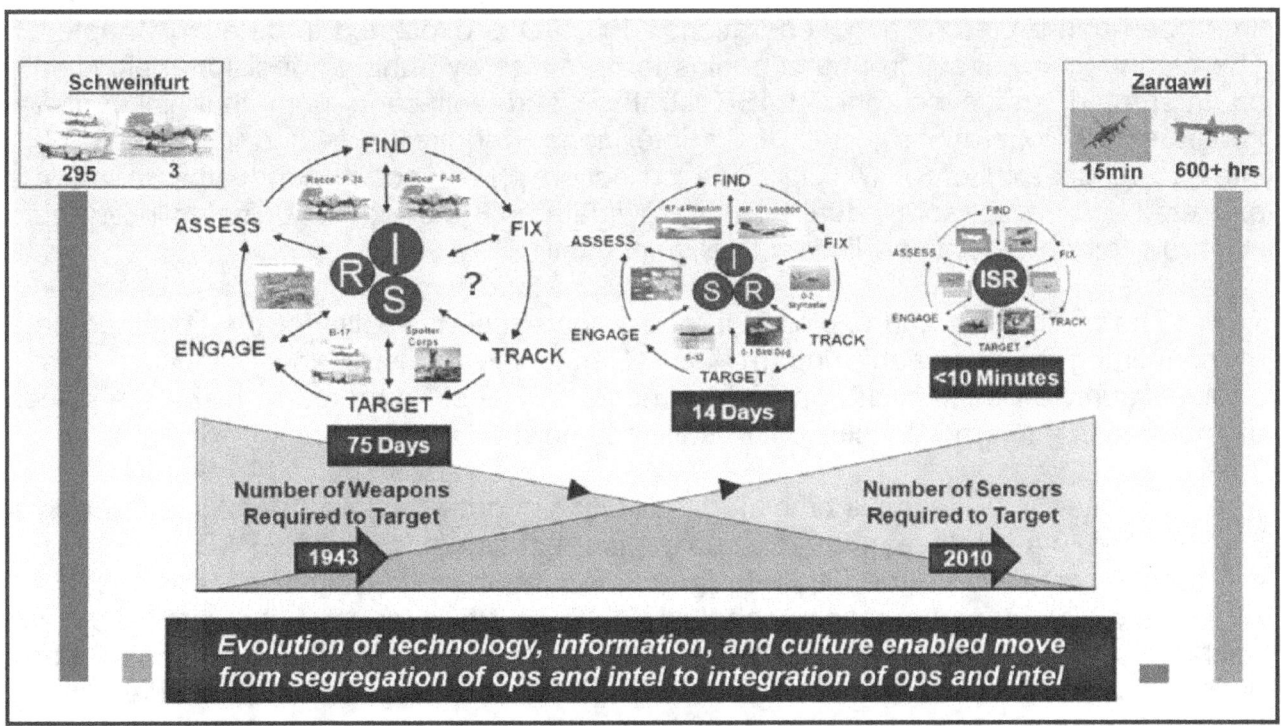

Figure 1.2. Information in War Revolution

Air Force global integrated ISR operations enable joint operations throughout the range of military operations (ROMO) in uncontested, contested, and denied environments by serving as a theater capability and facilitate the integration and synchronization of joint, defense, national, and coalition ISR capabilities. Other Services may focus organic elements of ISR efforts towards the tactical level of war, specifically in support of organic component operations (i.e., supporting a specific mission or unit). These forces are typically organic to a service echelon.

The Air Force currently uses the majority of its ISR assets to directly support national objectives and the joint force commander's (JFC's) strategic and operational goals. One of the most valuable attributes of airpower is its flexibility, the inherent ability to project power dynamically across large swaths of an operational area. Flexibility of ISR operations is exponentially enhanced with distributed ops. AF global integrated ISR monitors both friendly and adversary movements and capabilities in a dynamic environment, and drives the Find, Fix, Track, Target, Engage, and Assess process. However, the Air Force may designate some assets as organic assets to satisfy service-specific collection requirements. An example is the utilization of remotely piloted aircraft (RPA) to support base defense or special operations or cyberspace sensors to protect the AF network.

The Air Force conducts global integrated ISR operations through a five-phase process: planning and direction; collection; processing and exploitation; analysis and production; and dissemination (PCPAD). The process is not linear or cyclical, but rather represents a network of interrelated, simultaneous operations that can, at any given time, feed and be fed by other operations. PCPAD is explained in detail in Chapter 3. The planning and direction phase begins the process by shaping decision-making with an integrated and synchronized ISR strategy and collection plan that links global integrated ISR operations to the JFC's intelligence requirements and integrating them into the air tasking order (ATO). The collection phase occurs when the mission is executed and the sensors actually gather raw data on the target set. The collected data in its raw form has relatively limited intelligence utility.

The processing and exploitation phase increases the utility of the collected data by converting it into useable information. During the analysis and production phase analysts apply critical thinking and advanced analytical skills by fusing disparate pieces of information and draw conclusions resulting in finished intelligence.

Finished intelligence is crucial to facilitating informed decision-making, but only if it is received in a timely manner. Dissemination, the final phase of PCPAD, ensures the commander receives the derived intelligence in time to make effective decisions. The Air Force's distributed operations capability enables it to conduct global integrated ISR operations and provide timely and tailored intelligence on a global level to multiple end users. The analyzed intelligence can be disseminated or stored for future use. Under the Intelligence Community Directive 501, properly formatted and archived data in the evolving Library of National Intelligence will add to the ISR arsenal by making previously collected and exploited information readily available to correlate and provide context to data.

GLOBAL INTEGRATED ISR AS A SERVICE CORE FUNCTION

SCFs define the Air Force's key capabilities and contributions as a service. SCFs correspond to the specific primary functions of the Service as described in DoDD 5100.01. Synchronized with land and maritime ISR, Global integrated ISR enables the Air Force to deliver Global Vigilance, Global Reach, and Global power through cross-domain ISR integration–from, in and through air, space, and cyberspace.[2] "Our focus needs to be not on platforms but on providing optimal, maximized and seamless ISR capabilities, and that is where we are headed in our Air Force."[3]

BASIC GLOBAL INTEGRATED ISR PRINCIPLES

Global integrated ISR operations provide intelligence to commanders and decision-makers at all levels, informing the decision making process. Therefore, global integrated ISR operations and products should be responsive to the commander's or decision-maker's needs. Tailorable products enable strategic, operational, and tactical effects with a better understanding of the operational environment (systematically, spatially, and temporally); allowing decision-makers and warfighters to better orient themselves to the current and predicted situation and enable decisive action.

As an essential element of all Air Force operations, global integrated ISR linked personnel should be fully aware of mission goals and objectives and be integrated into the operational environment at all levels. This includes being integrated at the tactical level to ensure that global integrated ISR operations are included in supported force planning. Therefore, Global integrated ISR operations and the Joint Operation Planning Process (JOPP) need to be **integrated** to meet the timeliness and accuracy requirements of airpower and joint operations. A close relationship between the strategy, planning, assessment, and execution functions fosters the flow of essential information.

Global integrated ISR-derived products should be as **accurate** as possible to convey an appreciation for facts and the situation as it actually exists, and provide the best possible estimate of the enemy situation and courses of action (COAs) based on sound judgment of all available information. Extensive knowledge of adversary strategy, tactics, capabilities, and culture enables intelligence personnel to anticipate potential actions and provides the most complete and precise understanding of the adversary possible. Accuracy of geopositional data in intelligence products is a crucial requirement for targeting, particularly given increasing reliance on the use of precision-guided munitions. Sensors acquire information that enables targeteers to produce target locations or aim points suitable for the accurate employment of specific weapon systems. One of the most demanding tasks for global integrated ISR personnel during emerging crises is the need to balance requirements for accuracy and timeliness.

---

[2] Global Integrated ISR Service Core Function, Aug 2010.
[3] Lt Gen David Deptula, Former DCS for ISR

Global integrated ISR products need to be **relevant**, meaning that they are tailored to the requestor's requirements. Ensuring the relevance of intelligence to the requestor means that global integrated ISR planners should consider the suitability of specific ISR assets to achieve the commander's objectives. Additionally, global integrated ISR requirements should be **timely** enough to plan and execute operations. Intelligence resulting from timely global integrated ISR can provide information to aid a commander's decision-making and constantly improve the commander's understanding of the operational environment. The active nature of Air Force ISR assets makes them an essential enabler of timeliness when assets are made available to collect information when and where required. However, since availability of ISR assets is limited, responsiveness of ISR assets is often driven by the commander's objectives and priorities. Commanders must ensure proper asset utilization based on prioritized mission requirements. As technology evolves, every effort should be made to streamline processes to shorten timelines from tasking through product dissemination.

Global integrated ISR-derived information must be readily **accessible** to be usable. First, intelligence should be easily discoverable and retrievable; intelligence personnel must be able to "get at the information" in order to process, exploit, analyze, or disseminate. Second, producers and consumers should have the appropriate clearances to access and use the information. Third, global integrated ISR products should always be classified, catalogued, and electronically stored at the lowest possible classification, consistent with security policies, to enable sharing with partner nations, allies, interagency partners, and others. Understandably, some intelligence requires extraordinary protection, such as sensitive sources and methods, or the fact that certain knowledge is held.

Personnel working with classified material must **secure** and protect data, information and sensitive sources while informing commanders and their staffs. Protection of classified information and sources must be consistent with established DOD and Intelligence Community policies and procedures, especially when operations are conducted with coalition partners. Criteria, authority, and procedures for declassifying and/or sanitizing intelligence should be available at appropriate levels. Declassification procedures should be exercised on a regular basis. Classification authorities should avoid over-classification and unnecessary compartmentalization that can prevent commanders and staff from accessing needed intelligence. If directives are too restrictive to meet current operational requirements, additional guidance or authorization from the appropriate classification authority should be requested.

Global integrated ISR supporting resources, activities, communications, capabilities, and capacity should be **redundant** to ensure support is available when needed. Important components of survivability include redundancy of critical intelligence, protection against the adversary's asymmetrical threats (e.g., ISR Mission Assurance) and information assurance (IA) measures. It is vital for all global integrated ISR systems to be **sustainable**. A system's ability to maintain the necessary level and duration of operations depends on ready forces and resources in sufficient quantities to support stated requirements. Global integrated ISR systems are unique by being able to provide both **deployable** capabilities as well as reachback capabilities that can provide support for expeditionary operations. Many ISR supporting assets can be rugged, small, and lightweight. Additionally, they should be easy to transport and set up and capable of immediate connectivity and interoperability. Extensive reachback support, such as through RPAs, Distributed Ground Stations, and national intelligence centers, provides the ability for accomplishing a multitude of PCPAD capabilities. Many ISR Airmen support global missions through the reachback support they provide from their home bases.

Assured **network centricity** is a key principle for all Air Force global integrated ISR efforts. It is technology and its employment that aids in the efficient exchange of actionable information to operators at all levels. Net-centric global integrated ISR capabilities enable users to provide tailored and actionable intelligence that increases situational awareness and fosters the capacity to conduct operations with increased flexibility and rapidity. Net-centric collaborative environments support creation of "virtual organizations" where personnel from numerous agencies around the world horizontally align as a team, focus analytic effort on a question, and deliver answers or recommended COAs. Such collaborative efforts are encouraged to make the most efficient and effective use of available resources.

Through various cyberspace-based ISR capabilities, a wide variety of detailed sensor data can be posted to compatible, joint intelligence information stores, and continually searched in order to cross-cue and refine operations. Strategic, operational, and tactical users employ tailored searches to gain access to the right information at the right time to enable operations. Ideally, both command and control (C2) and global integrated ISR planning systems access common databases to synchronize collection and operations requirements.

POLICY AND GUIDANCE

Information derived from global integrated ISR assets is used on a daily basis by senior leadership to formulate strategic policy and military plans/guidance. Global integrated ISR-derived information is also used to guide acquisition of future capabilities, develop and construct military campaigns, protect US interests, and deter aggression. Understanding the policy and guidance that drives global integrated ISR operations is key to the first phase of the PCPAD process.

The National Security Strategy (NSS)

The NSS provides policy context which cements US plans and actions by describing the security environment and a desired response. Faced with the current worldwide terrorist threat, this US strategy has evolved to include an unprecedented emphasis on homeland security and a deliberate shift toward prevention.

Global Integrated ISR directly flows from the NSS in that Air Force global integrated ISR operations support multiple national strategic goals. Key underpinnings of the NSS are to engage with other countries, counter violent extremism, counter the spread of nuclear and biological weapons, and maintain the security of the United States, its citizens, and US allies and partners.[4] Global integrated ISR contributes to these specific NSS goals on a daily basis. Information garnered from global integrated ISR is shared globally to both prevent future terrorist attacks and to diffuse regional conflicts.

The National Defense Strategy (NDS)

The 2008 NDS states that in order for the United States to achieve its stated objectives of strengthening alliances, building partnerships, reducing the proliferation of Weapons of Mass Destruction (WMD) and preventing attacks against the homeland and our allies/friends, an effort needs to be made to jointly integrate and unify endeavors. Global integrated ISR capabilities and information can be leveraged in support of national defense across the ROMO. Global integrated ISR information applies across Services and across agencies. Global integrated ISR contributes to the NDS on a daily basis in support of the objectives to defend the homeland, promote security, deter conflict, and win our nation's wars.[5] Through global integrated ISR operations, the NDS acts on these objectives and evaluates the strategic environment, challenges and risks.

The National Military Strategy (NMS)

The NMS provides the advice of the Chairman of the Joint Chiefs of Staff, developed in consultation with the Joint Chiefs of Staff (JCS) and the combatant commanders (CCDRs), to the President and Secretary of Defense (SecDef) on the strategic direction of the Armed Forces. It assesses the strategic environment and describes the military's role as an integral part of a national effort in achieving the President's national security objectives and priorities. The NMS also outlines critical objectives, tasks, force employment concepts, and capabilities necessary to execute the NDS.

The 2011 NMS states that the Joint Forces will perform full spectrum operations to secure, maintain, and assure unhindered domain access, global strike, rapid global mobility, globally integrated ISR, command and control and retain the ability to project power into distant, anti-access environments. Additionally, it specifies that the Joint Forces will pursue resilient architectures, space situational awareness, provide options for self-defense and reconstitution, maintain symmetric and asymmetric capabilities to deter adversaries, and train for operations in space-degraded environments.

---

[4] The National Security Strategy, May 2010.
[5] The National Defense Strategy, June 2008.

The National Intelligence Strategy (NIS)

The NIS sets out the following guiding principles: responsive and incisive understanding of global threats and opportunities, coupled with an agility that brings to bear the Community's capabilities. The NIS also affirms priorities to focus Intelligence Community (IC) plans and actions for the next four years, while providing direction to guide development of future IC capabilities. The NIS highlights areas that demand our attention, resources, and commitment. It also establishes the basis for accountability, in conjunction with an implementation plan, to ensure that the Community meets the goals of our strategy.

The Defense Intelligence Strategy (DIS)

The DIS sets out to improve its intelligence support to fulfill SecDef priorities to prosecute global threats to US national security interests. It emphasizes ISR capabilities that are integrated and synchronized to support combat operations and sets several strategic objectives and priorities.

CROSS-DOMAIN INTEGRATION AND GLOBAL INTEGRATED ISR

Global integrated ISR operations are conducted in, from, and through all domains (air, land, maritime, space and cyberspace), across all phases of operations along the ROMO, in uncontested, contested and denied environments. These operations focus on meeting the JFC's intelligence requirements within very complex operational environments. Integrated PCPAD capabilities include integration of cross-domain collection activities utilizing the full-spectrum of sensors (signals intelligence, radar, electro-optical, infra-red, human, ground, etc); integrated processing and exploitation and analysis and production activities in Air Operation Centers (AOCs), Air Force Distributed Common Ground System (DCGS), and national production centers; and integrated intelligence products disseminated to tactical, operational and strategic users. Ultimately, cross-domain integrated capabilities enable global integrated ISR forces to quickly analyze collected data, and feed the resulting intelligence—real-time in many instances—to warfighters.

Net Centric Operations

Global integrated ISR systems use networks, satellite communications, and datalinks to execute global integrated ISR missions. This net centric structure is known as distributed operations and requires that global integrated ISR operations be cross-domain integrated. For example, a single global integrated ISR mission may be collecting on maritime target sets; using an airborne platform; transmitting collected data over space-based satellite communications to analysts in another part of the world who are creating and disseminating intelligence products through cyberspace.

For this reason, an open and cyber-assured net-enabled architecture is essential to cross-domain integrated analysis and dissemination. This architecture brings the global capabilities of Air Force global integrated ISR to bear on any challenge. The processed data from collection platforms must move on global networks to multiple analysis sites for exploitation and further dissemination. The results should be stored in such a way that they are readily discoverable and retrievable by other members of the global integrated ISR community to improve the timeliness, depth and accuracy demanded by multiple customers. The Air Force global integrated ISR vision implements the DOD net-centric information sharing vision in which all global integrated ISR assets can be managed [6]as a single constellation.

INTELLIGENCE PREPARATION OF THE OPERATIONAL ENVIRONMENT (IPOE)

IPOE is a valuable methodology focusing ISR for the commander and the commander's supporting C2 elements by getting "inside" the enemy's decision-making cycle. Specifically, IPOE focuses on the threat environment and its effect on both friendly and enemy COAs. IPOE and intelligence preparation of the battlespace (IPB) are key tools for conducting analysis and production that directly supports planning and direction. IPOE/IPB results in the production of an intelligence estimate, potential adversary COAs, named areas of interest, and high-value targets, which are inputs to the JOPP, Joint Force Commander (JFC), and Joint Force Air and Space Component Commander (JFACC) planning and targeting processes. The IPOE process includes integrating analysis, production, collection management, and targeting processes to shape decision making and enable operations.

A large part of IPOE is defense and penetration analysis. Detailed threat analysis is critical for friendly force mission planning and defense suppression across all domains. IPOE assesses how the enemy doctrinally organizes, trains, equips and employs their forces against friendly force vulnerabilities. IPOE also assesses the cultural, social, religious, economic, and government elements of the country/region to determine the possible effects of enemy and friendly COAs on them.

Additionally, IPOE alerts decision-makers at all echelons of command to potential emerging situations and threats. JFC guidance provided during planning shapes the overall concept of operations, which in turn drives planning requirements for air, space, and cyberspace employment. The challenge of the JFACC/Commander, Air Force Forces (COMAFFOR) is determining where and when to focus attention in order to influence events early, ready forces, and begin setting conditions for future operations. Therefore, preparation of the operational environment is essential to supporting the commander's visualization process, determining (component-level) intelligence requirements, anticipating critical decision points during operations, and prescribing rules of engagement (ROE).

IPOE plays an essential role in military operations across all domains by contributing to the Operational Preparation of the Environment (OPE)—those enabling functions conducted within all domains to plan and prepare for potential follow-on

---

[6] 2010 USAF ISR Strategy.

military operations. For example, Global integrated ISR provides the intelligence needed to understand how an adversary's networks can be affected by non-kinetic (cyberspace and information operations) capabilities. The global integrated ISR contribution to OPE includes but is not limited to identifying data, system/network configurations, or physical structures connected to or associated with the network or system, determining system vulnerabilities, and suggesting actions warfighters can take to assure future access and/or control of the system, network, or data during anticipated hostilities.

IPOE and target development processes highlight an adversary's centers of gravity (COGs), key capabilities and vulnerabilities, possible intentions, and potential COAs. By identifying known adversary capabilities, IPOE provides the conceptual basis for the JFC/JFACC/COMAFFOR to visualize how the adversary might threaten friendly forces or influence mission accomplishment. IPOE is the process in which critical thinking skills are applied to effectively counter an adversary's denial and deception strategy and anticipate surprise. Ultimately, IPOE shapes the JOPP.

CHAPTER TWO

COMMAND AND ORGANIZATION OF GLOBAL INTEGRATED ISR FORCES

We have taken huge leaps in terms of overall ISR capability. But the appetite continues to outpace as we understand more and more what it can do.

—Admiral Michael G. Mullen
Former Chairman, Joint Chiefs of Staff

Global integrated ISR operations are conducted across the ROMO. The Air Force organizes, trains, and equips forces to be employed in accordance with combatant commander direction. CCDRs typically employ intelligence related assets (assigned or attached forces) through their intelligence (J2) staffs for day-to-day operations. When a joint task force (JTF) is created, the JFC integrates the actions of assigned, attached, and supporting ISR forces within the operational area. C2 of airborne ISR is usually delegated to the JFACC.

Global integrated ISR enables strategic, operational, and tactical operations to achieve desired effects to satisfy national and military objectives by providing integrated ISR to a diverse set of consumers. These consumers include but are not limited to national agencies; geographic, functional, or Service components; and unit-level decision makers.

ROLES OF COMMANDERS

Command relationships delineate the degree of authority commanders have over forces. Understanding these authorities and how they fit in the PCPAD process is critical for global integrated ISR operations. This chapter discusses global integrated ISR command relationships from the perspectives of CCDR, JFC, JFACC, COMAFFOR, and national leaders. It also describes the types of Air Force organizations that conduct or utilize global integrated ISR operations. Refer to AFDD 1, *Air Force Basic Doctrine*, and JP 1, *Doctrine for the Armed Forces of the United States*, for a detailed discussion of command relationships.

THE COMBATANT COMMANDER

The CCDR employs assigned and attached ISR forces to achieve national and theater objectives. If necessary the CCDR will coordinate with other combatant commands through the Global Force Management (GFM) process to use assets not normally assigned to his theater, or coordinate the cooperative use of assets to improve coverage. Based on guidance and direction from the CCDR, the CCDR's J2 and operations (J3) staff develop an overall theater collection strategy and posture for the execution of the ISR missions.

At the theater level, the geographic CCDR exercises collection management authority (CMA) for collection operations in his theater. CMA involves two complementary functions: **collection requirements management** (CRM), defining what targets intelligence systems should collect; and **collection operations management** (COM), specifying how to satisfy the requirement. CRM focuses on the requirements of the customer, is all-source oriented, and advocates what information is required for collection. The collection management functions drive the planning and direction phase of the PCPAD process.

The CCDR may delegate operational control (OPCON) or tactical control (TACON) over some theater ISR assets to subordinate commanders. The CCDR, however, retains the authority to validate and prioritize requirements that will be collected by theater ISR assets.

THE JOINT FORCE COMMANDER

The JFC provides direction for component commands to employ assigned forces to achieve campaign objectives. The JFC normally delegates OPCON of assigned/attached Air Force assets to the COMAFFOR or TACON of airborne ISR assets to the JFACC. The JFACC then is responsible for tasking these ISR assets to support combat operations via the ATO.

The JFC's staff is responsible for developing a collection strategy and execution posture for ISR missions and coordinating with national agencies. The JFC establishes priorities for ISR operations which align with national and theater objectives. The JFC J2 reviews, validates, and prioritizes all outstanding intelligence requirements, whether originating from the JFC J2 staff or a subordinate component. High priority, time-sensitive requirements are identified and pre-validated by the JFC for the JFACC to consider for dynamic retasking during execution of ISR operations. Additionally, CCDR's and JFC's staffs produce theater plans, such as operations plans (OPLAN) and concept plans (CONPLAN), and tailors joint operational area (JOA) ISR assets to meet crisis requirements. The JFC may retain CRM responsibilities and delegate the responsibility for COM for the JOA to the supported commander for theater ISR, which is typically the JFACC or may be the COMAFFOR if no JFACC has been designated. It is the Air Force's position that the COMAFFOR, when dual-hatted as JFACC, is uniquely positioned to execute COM of assigned air, space, and cyberspace capabilities in the operational area (OA). As the supported commander for theater ISR the JFACC/COMAFFOR can leverage the AOC, and its C2 mechanism, to integrate CRM and COM.

With any command relationship pertaining to ISR forces, care should be taken to understand and align Title 10, United States Code (USC) and Title 50, USC authorities to avoid potential conflicts of interest or authorities. Placing the ISR organizations in support of a JFC often maintains this integrity by ensuring Title 10/Title 50 command lines are coherent. The supported commander then communicates and prioritizes requirements to enable adequate ISR support.

The JFC's staff is responsible for development of a federated architecture for intelligence exploitation and analysis, leveraging the support of organic capabilities at the component and JTF level, other CCDRs, and national agencies to ensure complete coverage of all requirements. Finally, in conjunction with functional and service components and coalition partners, the JFC requests ISR capabilities (personnel, platforms, etc.) to support current and planned requirements that exceed assigned/attached capabilities.

THE COMMANDER, AIR FORCE FORCES

The CCDR normally delegates OPCON over assigned/attached Air Force forces to the COMAFFOR. Of note, the COMAFFOR always holds administrative control (ADCON) over Air Force forces via the Service chain of command. The JFC typically designates the COMAFFOR as the JFACC.

If the JFC elects not to designate a JFACC, the COMAFFOR typically serves as the supported commander for theater ISR. During operations, collection managers (CMs) communicate the COMAFFOR's taskings through scheduling messages and by assembling a prioritized list of collection objectives. The COMAFFOR tasks attached and assigned airborne, space, and cyberspace capabilities via the ATO and CMs assemble a prioritized list of collection objectives for sensor use. Specific collection taskings are captured in the reconnaissance, surveillance, and target acquisition (RSTA) annex to the ATO which is guided by the ISR strategy developed during the Joint Air Operations Plan (JAOP) process.

THE JOINT FORCE AIR COMPONENT COMMANDER

The authority and command relationships of the JFACC are established by the JFC. Typically, the JFACC serves as the supported commander for theater airborne ISR and provides ISR for the JFC. The JFC normally delegates TACON of assigned, attached, and apportioned ISR assets (except those organic to other components) to the JFACC who will allocate them to support operations via the ATO. Additionally, the JFACC will exercise TACON, as delegated by the JFC, of all Air Force forces assigned or attached, and over those assets made available for tasking by the other Services. In short, the JFACC's responsibility is to satisfy the JFC's requirements.

The JFACC usually exercises authority through a joint or combined AOC. The joint air operations center (JAOC) is in the best location to fully integrate and C2 ISR assets and act as a broker to fulfill the JFC's ISR objectives. Additionally, the COMAFFOR, when designated as the JFACC, is the supported commander for theater ISR, as well as the area air defense commander (AADC), the airspace control authority (ACA), and the space coordinating authority (SCA). Each of these functions demands integration to ensure unity of command and effort.

If the JFACC does not have the available assets or capabilities to satisfy supported force requirements, the ISR division (ISRD) within the JAOC will identify those requirements and forward them to the JFC via the JFACC for resolution. Regardless of how the information is gathered, the JFACC must remain aware of all capabilities that can be integrated into ISR operations.

THEATER J2 RESPONSIBILITIES

Most often, joint task forces are organized with a combination of Service and functional component commands. The theater J2 should remain informed of all ISR requirements being levied on assets and resources within the CCDR's area of responsibility (AOR). The theater J2 retains full management authority (i.e., to validate, to modify, or to non-concur) over all theater ISR requirements within the AOR. The theater J2 executes these responsibilities through the Joint Intelligence Operations Center (JIOC).

Tasking and employment of any ISR asset required to support more than one JTF commander is coordinated and deconflicted by a common superior commander to the JTF commanders.

DEPARTMENT OF DEFENSE

The DOD develops the annual global theater ISR allocation plan and provides ISR sourcing recommendations in response to CCDR emergent requests and national intelligence requirements. In addition, PCPAD capacity is aligned with ISR allocation. Gaps in capability and shortfalls in capacity are identified. Furthermore, DOD also develops strategies and plans integrating and synchronizing the employment of national, DOD, and international partner capabilities.

HEADQUARTERS AIR FORCE (HAF) A2, DEPUTY CHIEF OF STAFF OF THE AIR FORCE FOR ISR

The Deputy Chief of Staff (DCS) of the Air Force for ISR, AF/A2, assists the Secretary of the Air Force and Chief of Staff in accomplishing the global integrated ISR mission of the Department of the Air Force. Most importantly, the AF/A2 serves as the HAF focal point responsible for functional management of all Air Force global integrated ISR capabilities; developing and implementing the Air Force policies and guidance for developing and managing Air Force global integrated ISR activities; and leading the organization, planning, and programming of Air Force ISR. Additional responsibilities of the DCS for ISR include oversight of planning, programming, and budgeting; professional development, training, education, readiness, and deployment of Air Force intelligence personnel; and advocacy for acquisition of global integrated ISR systems.

The DCS for ISR is the Air Force's Senior Intelligence Officer (SIO), representing the Air Force to national Intelligence Community (IC) through the Office of the Director of National Intelligence (ODNI). As the SIO for a designated IC organization, the DCS for ISR is responsible for integrating as well as leveraging AF and national capabilities, collaborating and sharing information while protecting the integrity of the intelligence process, and with establishing the necessary linkages between planning and execution for integrated AF and IC capabilities. The DCS for ISR must also evaluate and reconcile the intelligence budget for the AF and IC in light of established priorities and guidance. Further, the DCS for ISR formulates the Air Staff position on AF ISR matters under consideration by the JCS and National Security Council (NSC) and serves as the single point of contact in HAF. As such, the DCS for ISR is the principal AF advisor to national-level and DOD-level executive forums focusing on effectively integrating ISR programs and capabilities.

AIR FORCE ISR AGENCY (AFISRA)

AFISRA is a field operating agency subordinate to AF/A2. It is responsible for executing AF/A2's globally integrated ISR responsibilities. AFISRA organizes, trains, equips, presents assigned forces and integrates their all-source intelligence capabilities to the Air Force, CCDRs and the nation. AFISRA also acts as the Air Force Cryptologic Component under the National Security Agency (NSA)/Central Security Service and the AF GEOINT Element Commander. As AF DCGS lead, AFISRA manages all distributed operations. When Air Force component intelligence requirements exceed the theater's capabilities, AFISRA may reinforce the combatant command with analytical capability.

AIR FORCE COMPONENT A2

As the Air Force Service component commander for the joint force, the COMAFFOR is responsible for presenting Air Force global integrated ISR capabilities to the JFC. The COMAFFOR's A2 directs Air Force intelligence forces by recommending policy and guidance and ensuring coordination among various intelligence functions. The A2 is responsible for intelligence plans and programs, sensitive compartmented information management, intelligence liaison, foreign disclosure and intelligence information management functions.[7] The intelligence structure should be designed to expedite tailored intelligence to operational units. The A2 exercises day-to-day

---

[7] AFI 14-202v3, *General Intelligence Rules*

responsibility for intelligence support to the COMAFFOR and assigned/attached Air Force forces (AFFOR). This includes the following:

○ Serves as Air Force forces SIO. Advises the COMAFFOR on all intelligence matters impacting mission accomplishment.

○ Recommends Air Force intelligence policy and guidance for operations within the JOA.

○ Establishes, coordinates, and monitors AFFOR ISR requirements and capabilities to support operations in the JOA. Coordinates and monitors JFC global integrated ISR requirements.

○ Coordinates with JFC staff to establish relationships governing federated global integrated ISR operations and distributed operations in theater.

○ Validates unit intelligence and systems requirements and manages fielding and operation of automated intelligence systems.

○ Participates in the contingency planning processes and development of services annexes to CONPLANs, OPLANs, planning orders (PLANORDS), and operation orders (OPORDs).

○ Assists the A3/5 in developing the Air Force component commander's critical information requirements (CCIRs). Plans and develops implementing instructions for wartime intelligence support including augmentation of joint forces.[8]

○ Plans intelligence architecture support to satisfy Service-specific weapon system employment requirements in accordance with theater/JOA OPLANS.

○ Establishes procedures for and manages theater/JOA production requests and requests for information (RFIs).

○ Validates, prioritizes, and sources unit requirements for intelligence information.

THE ISR DIVISION

The ISRD of the AOC integrates the JFC's theater-wide global integrated ISR capabilities, to include distributed support. Central functions of the ISRD include planning, collection management and analysis. The ISRD is responsible for effectively orienting the COMAFFOR/JFACC to current and emerging enemy capabilities, threats, COAs, COGs, global integrated ISR operations management and targeting intelligence support. The ISRD accomplishes this task by integrating the Joint ISR and ATO

---

[8] AFI 14-202v3, *General Intelligence Rules*

processes. Within the AOC, the ISRD provides intelligence crucial to the air mobility, strategy, combat plans, and combat operations divisions that are planning and executing theater-wide operations. This intelligence helps achieve the commander's objectives as well as provides the means by which the effects of the operations are measured.

The ISRD has primary responsibility to support the planning, tasking, and execution of theater air, space, and cyberspace global integrated ISR operations. The ISRD serves as the senior intelligence element of the theater air control system (TACS), and as such integrates global integrated ISR platforms and capabilities (internal and external to the AOC) in support of the joint force. Additionally, the ISRD ensures that global integrated ISR is optimally managed to operate within the context of a complex national and joint intelligence architecture.

The ISRD Chief is the SIO for the AOC and reports to the AOC Director. As such, the ISRD Chief works in close coordination with other Division Chiefs and senior AOC staff to determine the best utilization of ISR personnel throughout the AOC to support AOC processes and requirements. The ISRD Chief ensures that the ISR Division:

✪ Provides analyses of the enemy and a common threat picture to the JFACC, staff planners, AOC divisions and other Air Force elements in theater.

✪ Provides combat ISR support assessment activities for air, space, and information operations planning and execution. Of note, this activity is normally accomplished in conjunction with the strategy, combat plans, and combat operations divisions.

✪ Directs the AOC's air, space, and cyberspace global integrated ISR operations, to include distributed operations.

✪ Provides direct targeting support to the ATO cycle in response to JFACC guidance.

✪ Provides all-source intelligence support to other AOC divisions to enhance the execution of their core processes.

ISRD and PCPAD
The ISRD is key in all of the elements of the PCPAD process. Two of the central functions of the ISRD in the PCPAD process are collection management and analysis.

Collection Management
The ISRD's collection management function is key to the success of global integrated ISR operations. Its responsibilities span all aspects of global integrated ISR operations, including RFIs and collection requirements management, global integrated ISR mission tasking, planning, and execution, and global integrated ISR and combat assessment (CA) activities. More specifically, ISRD CMs deal with JFACC/COMAFFOR priority intelligence requirements (PIRs), RFIs, and collection

requirements, which drive global integrated ISR operations. After vetting from the analysis function, the CM function determines whether the RFI should become a collection requirement or continue to a higher echelon as an RFI. Of note, CMs are responsible for consolidating, validating, and prioritizing subordinate unit and JFACC collection requirements submitted to the JFC for validation and collection. Collection managers are responsible for advocating JFACC intelligence requirements to the JFC J2. The process for developing and validating ISR collection requirements is essentially the same during peacetime, crisis, and war—only the nature of the requirements and the timeliness in which they should be satisfied varies. It is the Air Force's position that the AOC, specifically the ISRD, is the best location for COM of airborne global integrated ISR operations to be handled within the OA.

Within the AOC, the ISRD plans air, space, and cyberspace global integrated ISR operations in conjunction with the Strategy and Combat Plans Divisions, while the Combat Operations Division executes the ISR operations in concert with other key Air Force, joint, other government agencies, and coalition partners. Collection managers coordinate with operations planners to determine if service components' organic assets are capable of satisfying a specific requirement. If organic assets are available, then the appropriate unit will be tasked by the proper authority who exercises OPCON or TACON over that particular collection asset. Most importantly, CMs should seek to maximize the use of existing collections; this requires full access to national databases. For the remaining collection requirements, the JFC J2 will adjudicate competing component requirements and produce the Joint Integrated Prioritized Collection List (JIPCL). A portion of the JIPCL is then assigned to the JFACC for airborne collection. Collection managers then schedule and execute these collection requirements assigned to the JFACC via the ATO RSTA annex, and may collaborate with other key Air Force, joint, other government agencies, and coalition partners on non-airborne ISR requirements. CMs are responsible for ISR assessment and ISR employment recommendations to the JFACC, theater functional components, and the JFC, as applicable.

The ISRD collection management function also works extensively with targeteers and the Strategy Division to provide global integrated ISR combat assessment activities for air, space, cyberspace and information operations planning and execution. ISRD CMs are responsible to provide feedback to the JFC J2 on the theater requirements management process.

Analysis

AF analysts are a highly trained work force using best analytical techniques and processes to provide decision advantage and assure US national security. They synthesize data, apply critical thinking, and conduct predictive analysis in order to provide accurate IPOE/IPB, intelligence estimates and other products. AF analysts are employed at all echelons and across the Joint/coalition community. For example, they provide advice to the JFC, JFACC, staff planners, AOC divisions and other elements which shape the JOPP. They are also integral to JIOC organizations. Analysts ensure fused threat information from all sources is depicted in common operational pictures

(COP) and provide this picture as inputs to the JFC and JFACC planning, intelligence collection, and targeting processes. Additionally, analysts ensure that this information is coordinated with national, joint, component, and theater entities.

Specifically, AF analysts within the unit support cell are responsible for ensuring dissemination of JFACC, component, and joint theater intelligence products (as required) to Air Force and other Joint/coalition units. Unit support personnel also receive and integrate intelligence reporting in the form of mission reports (MISREPs) from Air Force air, space, and cyberspace units. The unit support cell also receives RFIs from air units assigned or attached to the JFACC and coordinates that request with the RFI management cell.

AOC ISR PERSONNEL BEYOND THE ISRD

Air Force ISR personnel are embedded throughout the AOC divisions and staff elements with the sole purpose of integrating global integrated ISR throughout the Air, Space, and Cyberspace planning cycle and to support command and control of theater air, space, and cyberspace forces. In general, assigned ISRD personnel provide tailored analytical and targeting products to each element, and manage intelligence requirements supporting global integrated ISR operations.

The Combat Operations Division (COD)
The COD is responsible for executing "today's war." ISR personnel within the Combat Ops Division form the Senior Intelligence Duty Officer (SIDO) Team which is responsible for providing up-to-date intelligence inputs in order to provide maximum situational awareness for the Chief of Combat Operations. SIDO responsibilities include leading a team responsible for current global integrated ISR operations. This team maintains an accurate threat picture, supports dynamic operations (i.e., personnel recovery and prosecution of dynamic targets), and monitors execution of the ATO and RSTA annex governing global integrated ISR operations.

The SIDO Team is also responsible, through close coordination with platform and processing, exploitation and dissemination (PED) liaison officers (LNOs), for dynamic retasking of theater air, space, and cyberspace global integrated ISR assets and requisite PED support for JFC objectives.

The Combat Plans Division
The Combat Plans Division is responsible for translating operational level guidance into tactical air, space, and cyberspace planning through the ATO process. Personnel enable theater air, space, and cyberspace operations by ensuring that global integrated ISR actions are clearly linked to the Commander's objectives. ISRD analysts provide continually updated IPOE analysis, and generate RFIs as needed to respond to specific requirements of the ATO planning process. Targeteers assist in validation of all targets for inclusion in the draft Joint Integrated Prioritized Target List (JIPTL) consistent with objectives, guidance, ROE, and in accordance with the Law of Armed Conflict (LOAC).

ISR planners ensure integration of global integrated ISR operations into the ATO process by coordinating ISR asset inclusion in the Master Air Attack Plan (MAAP) and the RSTA annex which focuses priorities, weight of effort, and intended goals.

The Strategy Division

The Strategy Division is responsible for the long-term operational level planning and assessment of theater air, space, and cyberspace operations. Intelligence personnel in the Strategy Division assist in developing the overall air component strategy, JAOP, and Air Operations Directive (AOD). Assigned analysts provide IPOE products, coordinate with global integrated ISR teams to develop JFACC PIRs, and ensure PIRs are included in the JAOP and AOD. Collection experts provide advice on available ISR assets, capabilities, and develop the JFACC ISR strategy as part of the overall air component strategy. Strategy Division targeteers use global integrated ISR products to provide Target System Analysis (TSA) and coordinate to assist in developing the objectives, tasks, and measure of effectiveness (MOE) which form the foundation of the combat assessment process. Likewise, targeteers also provide combat assessment inputs (contributing to Battle Damage Assessment (BDA), Munitions Effectiveness, and Mission Assessment), feeding the ATO cycle.

The Air Mobility Division (AMD)

The AMD is responsible for planning and executing intra-theater airlift operations and integrating inter-theater airlift operations conducted in the theater. Assigned ISR personnel provide tailored intelligence supporting theater mobility operations, and provide necessary reachback to ISR operations support conducted by the 618th Air and Space Operations Center[9] at Air Mobility Command.

CENTERS OF EXCELLENCE

Much of today's intelligence support comes from dedicated Centers of Excellence. Centers of Excellence respond to Air Force requirements for analysis in specialized areas of knowledge and practice. As directed by Air Force senior leaders, Centers of Excellence provide focused research, lessons-learned, education, outreach and support. Centers serve the needs of Airmen, leaders and the Air Force organizations responsible for policy, doctrine, training and specialized military roles. Centers also provide intelligence support to national intelligence organizations (Defense Intelligence Agency (DIA), NSA, National Geospatial Intelligence Agency (NGA), etc.) and national policymakers, responsible for using such information to make strategic and policy decisions. Global integrated ISR professionals are integrated into these centers to provide timely, relevant, and focused intelligence to support center objectives.

These centers provide specific expertise that can be leveraged by the COMAFFOR and AOC when they lack resources or required expertise. Some

---

[9] Tanker Airlift Control Center.

examples of centers of excellence are: National Air and Space Intelligence Center (the Air Force and DOD Center of Excellence for all-source air and space intelligence), Air Force Targeting Center (Center of Excellence for geospatial intelligence, target analysis and precision engagement intelligence), 688th Information Operations Wing, the USAF Expeditionary Operations School (Air Force Expeditionary Combat Support Center of Excellence), and Air Force Cyberspace Technical Center of Excellence.

DESIGNATED ISR WINGS, GROUPS AND SQUADRONS

Air Force ISR Wings perform a variety of functions. Specific global integrated ISR functions may include the production of tailored intelligence for weapons systems acquisition, mission planning and targeting, collection management, logistics and readiness issues, and communications/computer system support. Additionally, some ISR Groups have specific operational missions that relate to C2; acquisition/research and development; space surveillance; threat warning and technical analysis; Signals Intelligence (SIGINT) oriented cryptologic support; and scientific and technical intelligence (S&TI) support.

ISR squadrons collect, process, exploit, and disseminate intelligence in response to taskings from national authorities, theater commanders, and the JFACC. ISR squadrons conduct various missions including military capabilities and Order of Battle (OB) analysis, unit support, targeting support, Human Intelligence (HUMINT), Geospatial Intelligence (GEOINT) and SIGINT collection, processing, exploitation, and dissemination.

WING, GROUP & SQUADRON INTELLIGENCE SUPPORT

The primary focus of global integrated ISR at the operational wing, group, and squadron levels is the application of all-source intelligence information to sustain operations. Although the wing's intelligence capability is focused within a flight of the unit's Operations Group, intelligence personnel and assets are assigned to each operational squadron or may be attached to wing staffs. This capability supports unit deployments, readiness training, mission planning, and other wing-level mission functions. Most unit-level intelligence organizations are composed of two branches—operational intelligence (also termed "combat" intelligence) and target intelligence. Each performs a specific function. First, operational intelligence keeps the commander and operations crews informed of intelligence matters needed to perform the mission. It maintains intelligence database holdings, provides current threat briefings and training, and helps with mission planning. Second, target intelligence assembles and maintains mission or planning folders with related target planning documentation including imagery, maps, and navigation charts. Important global integrated ISR functions that may be performed at the unit level include:

✪ Mission planning and IPOE support.

- Defensive threat capabilities and penetration analysis.

- Mission folder construction and maintenance.

- Crew target study, mission planning, threat avoidance/defeat planning, and certification.

- Debriefing, assessment, weapons system recorded media exploitation, and intelligence reporting.

- Essential Elements of Information (EEI) and RFI management.

AIR CONTROL SQUADRONS

Air control squadrons provide long range and persistent surveillance, early warning, airspace control, and airborne battle management capabilities for operations across the spectrum of conflict. While these units do not generally produce raw data specifically designed for the global integrated ISR process, much of the information generated by these units is useful and can be fused with existing data to create a more accurate picture of the operational environment.

RECONNAISSANCE SQUADRONS

Reconnaissance squadrons are responsible for providing raw data for input into the PCPAD process. These units are responsible for providing national and theater command authorities with a wide array of timely, reliable, high-quality, reconnaissance products. Additionally, critical, perishable reconnaissance data can be routed directly to the shooter in near-real time. Reconnaissance data is often fused together with other intelligence to form a variety of global integrated ISR-related products which range from Indications and Warning (I&W) to long-range assessments of adversary capabilities.

SPACE OPERATIONS UNITS

Space operations units typically operate military and national-level assets, including ground-based radars, satellites, and other sensors, which collect information to support strategic-, operational-, and tactical-level decision-making. Forward units can access this data through tools and reachback processes. DIA coordinates requirements through NGA, National Reconnaissance Office (NRO) and NSA for tasking of national reconnaissance systems. For additional information on space operations, see AFDD 3-14, *Space Operations*.

MULTI-NATIONAL INTELLIGENCE OPERATIONS

Multinational operations are becoming the norm for military operations, making intelligence-sharing with allies and coalition partners increasingly important. In some multinational operations or campaigns, JFCs will be able to use existing international standardization agreements (STANAGs) (e.g., North Atlantic Treaty Organization (NATO) STANAGs) as a basis for establishing rules and policies for conducting joint intelligence operations. A JFC participating in a coalition or alliance should tailor procedures for that particular operation based on CCDR guidance and national policy as contained in National Disclosure Policy (NDP) 1, *National Policy and Procedures for the Disclosure of Classified Military Information to Foreign Governments and International Organizations*. NDP 1 provides policy and procedures in the form of specific disclosure criteria and limitations, definition of terms, release arrangements, and other guidance. The disclosure of classified information is never automatic. Any disclosure should be consistent with US national policy and US military objectives and be done with the assistance of a Foreign Disclosure Officer (FDO).

ISR SPECIAL RELATIONSHIPS

Global integrated ISR operations ultimately contribute to commanders' decision making, and its execution is a responsibility of command across the range of military operations. The functions of PCPAD specifically enable the commander and those charged with executing OPLANs across domains and Service entities. However, some service core functions and Air Force mission sets require that ISR operations emphasize the tenets of airpower according to particular mission sets. Special operations and nuclear operations are examples of mission sets where the global integrated ISR relationship is characterized by nuances in battle rhythms and time constraints.

Special Operations

Air Force Special Operations Forces (AFSOF) planning and execution are intelligence-intensive. Timely, detailed and global integrated ISR support is vital. In essence, intelligence requirements for AFSOF are similar to those of other air components, though the degree of detail is dramatically increased. Additionally, the nature of the objective may require tailored support. For instance, special operations forces (SOF) may require detailed global integrated ISR support in order to attack an objective (i.e., number of escape routes or time of day traffic analysis at objective). SOF global integrated ISR support tends to rely on organic assets, be less centralized and focused at the tactical level.

United States Special Operations Command (USSOCOM) has designated Air Force Special Operations Command (AFSOC) as the lead SOF component for RPA operations. AFSOC is also responsible for ISR PED operations supporting SOF and for oversight and tasking of conventional PED nodes when SOF PED requirements exceed organic capacity to satisfy.

Release of post-mission reports may be constrained by the sensitivity of many types of SOF missions. Depending on the sensitivity of the mission, commanders should report data either through special access or routine intelligence reporting channels, as appropriate.

Nuclear Operations

Nuclear operations require focused and detailed global integrated ISR during all stages of planning, execution, and assessment. ISR assets provide planners the data required to assess the threat environment, identify critical targets, determine appropriate weapons selection and provide essential post-strike assessments of both friendly and enemy situations. A key aspect of nuclear operations is the ability to survive in pre-, trans-, and post-strike environments associated with the unique nature of nuclear weapons. All-source ISR assets play a critical role in national decision-making by providing commanders the information to make timely decisions and enable civilian leaders to send timely and targeted deterrent signals to our adversaries and assurance to our allies.

PRESENTATION OF FORCES

Air Force global integrated ISR forces are presented to JFCs both inside and outside an Air Expeditionary Task Force (AETF) structure. For example, forces provided to a JTF (e.g., aircraft) and forces which support that mission (e.g., intelligence support) are presented as part of the AETF's organization.

However, the Air and Space Expeditionary Force (AEF) process has limitations when presenting global integrated ISR forces to the JFC. Requirements for collection, production, exploitation and dissemination components, and long-term analysis capabilities can vary by mission and area of operation. Therefore, these parts of the "global integrated ISR chain" cannot be pre-planned and adequately provided by the AEF process.

Air Force global integrated ISR forces are sometimes employed in support of other components through Joint Expeditionary Taskings (JET). These taskings are service-specific and are allocated based on Requests for Forces (RFFs) submitted by a CCDR. Several taskings/requirements necessitate a unique mix of skills. This requires Air Force global integrated ISR personnel be attached based on skill sets required to present that capability rather than an AETF. Because global integrated ISR forces are tasked based on capability, the request for forces from the sister Service needs to specify skill set and echelon requirements more than position and rank required. This provides the Air Force latitude in tailoring the makeup and size of the forces presented to provide optimum support.

Finally, the Air Force conducts considerable "peacetime" global integrated ISR operations in support of combatant commands or interagency customers which do not support a JTF and thus, do not fall under a particular AETF.

DISTRIBUTED OPERATIONS

A majority of Air Force global integrated ISR capabilities are provided to the JFC via distributed operations. Distributed operations allow for global integrated ISR capabilities to be presented with a reduced forward footprint. This puts fewer Airmen in harm's way without sacrificing operational effectiveness. The decision to establish distributed or split operations offers several tradeoffs. First, the fewer personnel/forces deployed forward, the less support is required. This may, however, limit face-to-face interaction between forward and rear decision-makers stretching decision-making timelines. Additionally, fewer personnel/forces forward also reduces security requirements. Yet, there is a possible void of expertise forward, forcing reachback coordination. Finally, reachback requires expanded communications infrastructure which may increase vulnerabilities. Still, it could be argued that distributed operations may be more survivable and less vulnerable to single-points of failure.

One of the most valuable attributes of airpower is its flexibility, the inherent ability to project power dynamically across large swaths of an operational area. Flexibility of ISR operations is exponentially enhanced when RPAs are operated via a C2 technique termed remote split operations (RSO). RPA RSO missions provide a unique capability to transition RPA aircrews between missions across the globe in minutes in response to dynamic and changing requirements. As a result, RSO provides national decision makers the means to dynamically translate strategic priorities into forces and capabilities, determine where the US military should be focused, and where the nation can afford to accept risk.

RSO, a critical element of distributed operations, employs forward-deployed, multi-role RPAs from home station via satellite links. The RSO approach has many inherent advantages. RSO reduces the deployed footprint at consolidated operating locations to only those forces required to launch, recover, and maintain aircraft. RSO does not require reconstitution of the RPAs at home station, enabling deployment of the vast majority of the RPA fleet. Thanks to RSO, the majority of the aircrew and associated personnel operate from home station and requires minimal reconstitution. Finally, asset consolidation at the forward location enables substantial maintenance efficiencies to be leveraged. While RSO decreases the need to forward deploy personnel for a given operation, it is important to note that RSO does not decrease the global requirement for RPA aircraft and aircrews or the global requirement for ISR personnel.

RSO of RPAs is a force multiplier for the joint force that produces unparalleled economy of force and delivers increased combat power during military operations. The dynamic flexibility provided by RSO enables optimal use of scarce resources, rapid response to changing mission requirements among multiple combatant commands, and highly capable global strike and globally persistent surveillance. Figure 2.1 depicts the AF ISR Enterprise's RPA global operations structure.

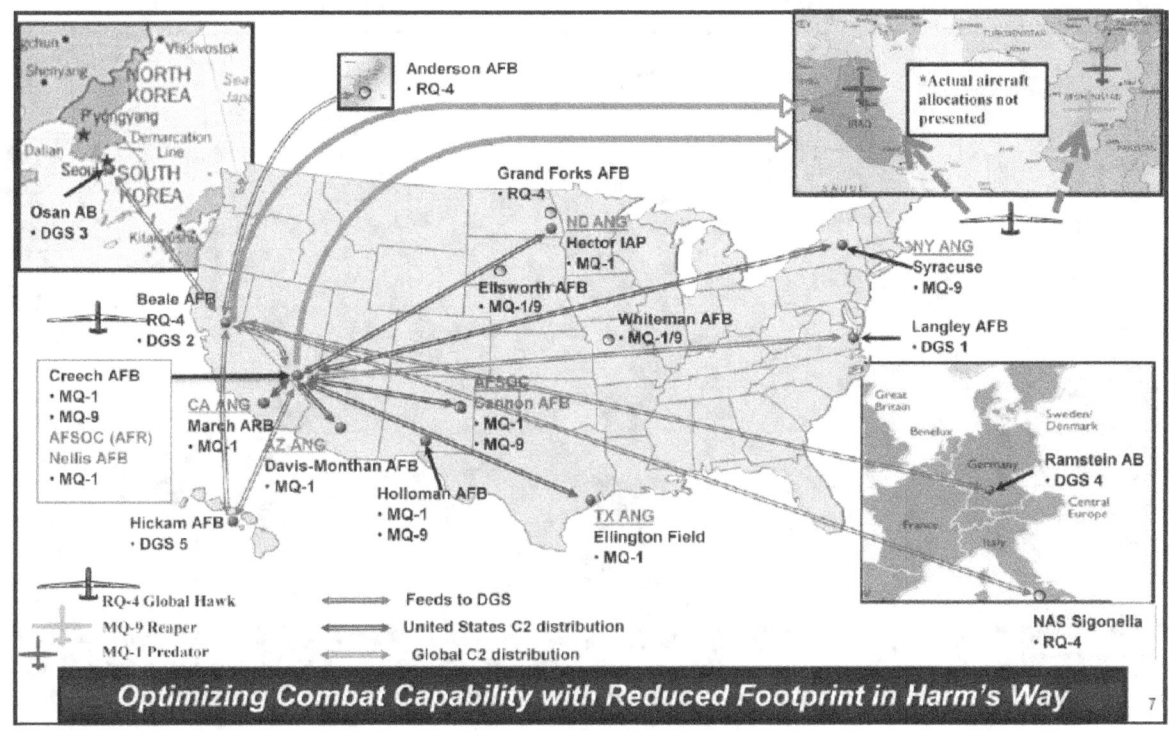

Figure 2.1. Remotely Piloted Aircraft Global Operations

DISTRIBUTED COMMON GROUND SYSTEM RESPONSIBILITIES/AUTHORITIES

The Air Force DCGS is a network-centric, global ISR enterprise. Its activities are tasked and managed to support CCDRs and forces—primarily at the JTF level and below—with actionable, decision-quality information, in accordance with established priorities as approved by the SecDef via the JS GFM process. The DCGS is the Air Force weapon system which provides PED for most Air Force airborne imagery intelligence (IMINT) and SIGINT collection. Air Force Distributed Ground Systems (DGSs) operate with the full flexibility of the established intelligence process, as detailed in JP 2-01, *Joint and National Intelligence Support to Military Operations*, in order to make usable information immediately and simultaneously available to both engaged forces and intelligence analysts. The Air Force has chosen to designate specific DGSs to focus regionally but still be able to support global operations as prioritized by SecDef. However, the strength of the DCGS system is that each DGS is networked and linked. Therefore, if one DGS requires support another DGS can help support the workload thereby maximizing the effectiveness of the entire enterprise while increasing efficiency by not duplicating manpower and other resources at each site. Figure 2.2 shows the AF DCGS Enterprise.

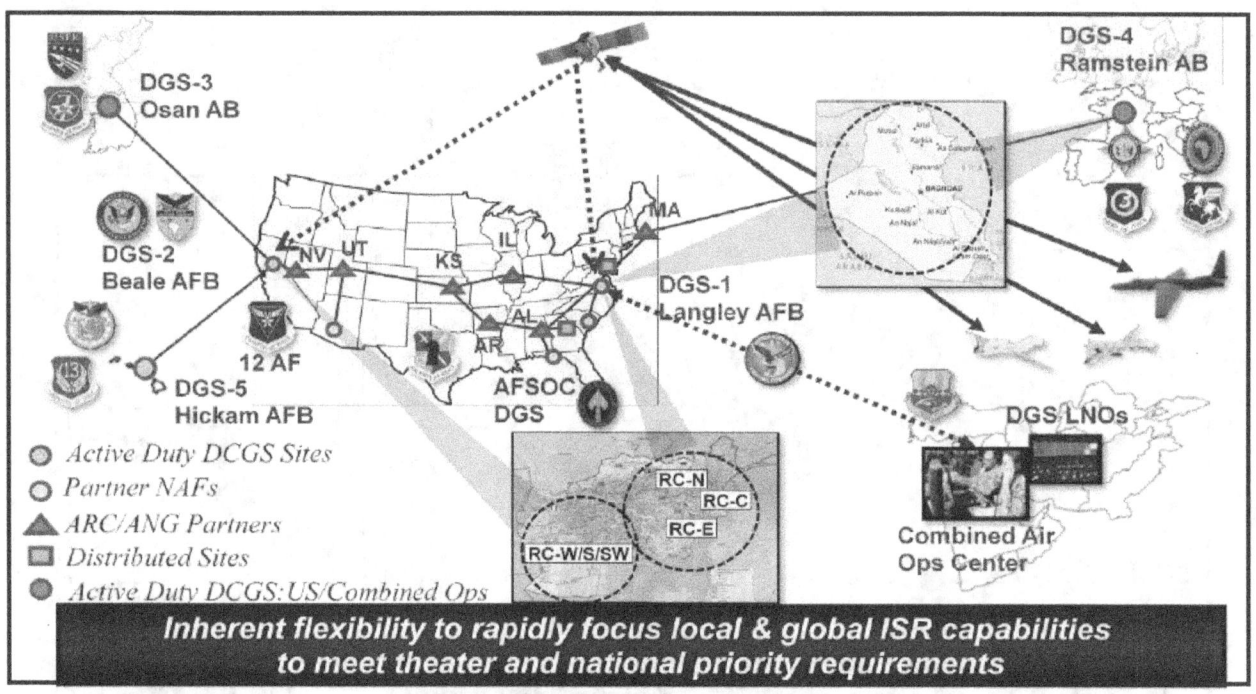

Figure 2.2. Air Force Distributed Common Ground System

SOF are supported by AFSOC's organic SOF DGS, a networked enterprise providing highly detailed intelligence products to fielded forces. This enterprise includes multiple DOD and national exploitation nodes, all focused on providing high quality, responsive intelligence to various levels of special operations entities deployed globally. This enterprise extensively leverages capabilities and products from the national intelligence community in support of SOF personnel.

Air Force DCGS takes advantage of Air Force, other Service, national, and coalition sensors in all domains and ingests information from all sources of intelligence. Air Force DCGS then provides products which are tailored for end-user requirements, in the formats, timelines, and channels required. Most importantly, the Air Force DCGS system is scalable and capable of both forward-based and globally distributed operations. Of note, the Air Force DCGS is a component of the larger DOD DCGS enterprise.

AFISRA executes global DCGS operations via the 480th ISR Wing, which commands seven ISR Groups to access the Air Force DCGS enterprise, and the 70th ISR Wing, which commands one ISR Group to support the DCGS. These groups, their associated Intelligence Support Squadrons, and DGSs are focused regionally to a Component Major Command (C-MAJCOM) or Component Numbered Air Force (C-NAF) and CCDR while also leveraging and supporting nationally tasked cryptologic missions.

Although ISR groups are aligned regionally and provide direct support to CCDRs, the power of DCGS is the ability to focus ISR capability where and when required based on DOD priorities. For example, a DCGS unit providing direct support to a regional theater can be directed to support another regional theater, in part or in whole, depending on the requirements levied upon it by higher DOD authorities. DCGS personnel support operations in air, space, and cyberspace. Figure 2.3 depicts the AF DCGS organizational structure.

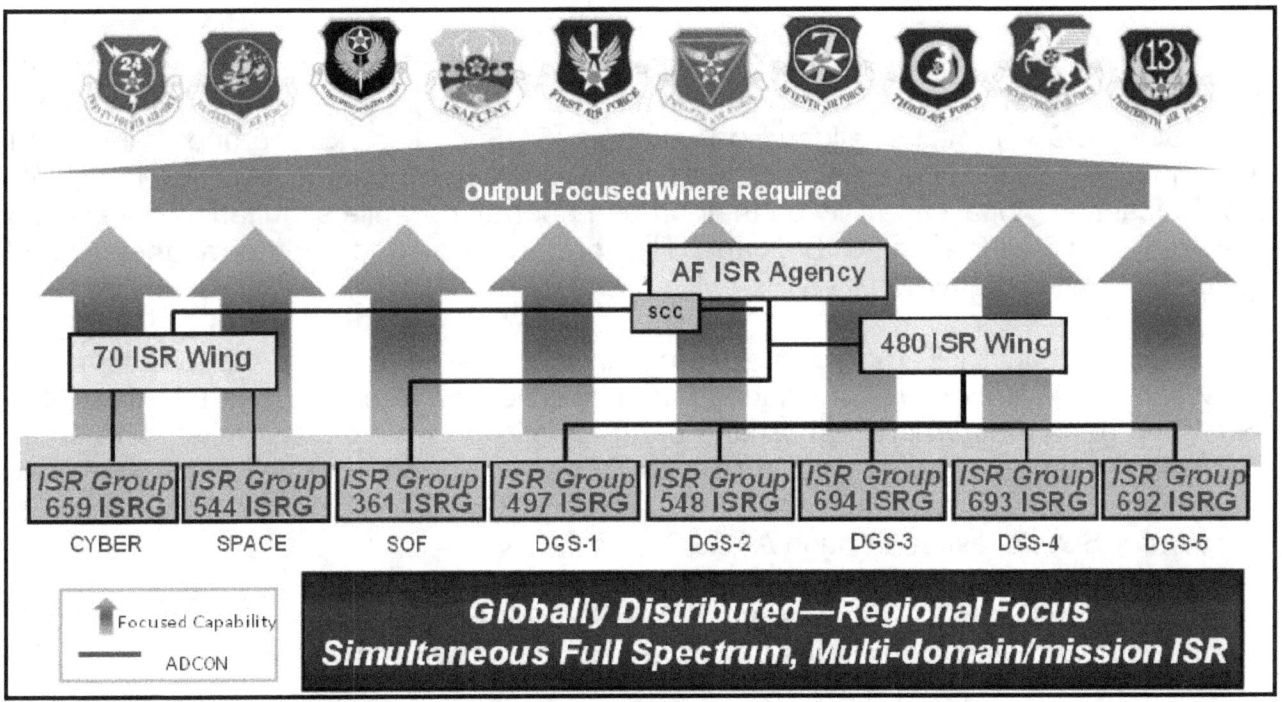

Figure 2.3. DCGS Organizational Structure

DCGS conducts ISR operations throughout the PCPAD process and across the full range of military operations, and does so in close coordination and partnership with reconnaissance squadrons and national intelligence agencies. ISR cross-cueing is one way DCGS operates. An example of cross-cueing would be a DCGS signals operator employing sensors aboard a U-2 on the other side of the planet to geo-locate a target signal and then cue a geospatial analyst working in the same room to coordinate with a Predator unit thousands of miles away to steer its video sensor to observe the source of the signal, and immediately report their findings directly to a supported unit in the area. SOF receive similar support through the SOF DGS enterprise, as executed by AFSOC.

DCGS provides operational ISR to all levels of war to achieve desired effects to accomplish commander objectives. The SOF DGS is specifically focused on providing very detailed, tailored intelligence products and reporting to SOF deployed globally.

Air Force DCGS PED will support the overall GFM Allocation Plan. AFISRA presents flexible Air Force DCGS PED capabilities to the CCDR or JFC via a net-centric environment. AFISRA continually presents the DCGS forces via the Total Force concept. The Total Force is comprised of Air Force active duty, Reserve, Air National Guard (ANG), civilian, and contractor personnel. AFISRA sites leverage locations around the globe using personnel from diverse units. Some Guard and Reserve units are designated Air Force DCGS nodes.

Once tasked, Air Force DCGS crews perform PCPAD to include ISR fusion. Air Force DCGS capabilities are not normally presented as part of an AETF due to the global integration of Air Force DCGS operations.

Each of the five Air Force DCGS core sites forms the operational base of the ISR groups, and each group is operationally aligned with a primary C-MAJCOM/C-NAF. The SOF DGS remains aligned to support SOF. The ISR groups and their accompanying architecture were created to possess the inherent flexibility to rapidly focus local and global capability on their area of operations while simultaneously shifting elements of global integrated ISR capability from one region to another as theater and national priorities require.

Conventional PED capabilities are primarily tasked via the supported theater ATO and RSTA annex which includes platform collection decks. From this the 480th ISR Wing generates an internal tasking order for all Air Force DCGS units. The 480th ISR Wing is the lead operational Air Force DCGS wing and operates the 480th Wing Operations Center (WOC) and the AF DCGS PED Operations Center (DPOC). PED support for SOF is tasked through AFSOC.

Once tasked, DCGS forces present flexible Air Force, Joint, and combined PED. The flexibility/strength of Air Force DCGS forces are enhanced by:

✪ **Logistics:** Presentation of Air Force DCGS capabilities does not require an extensive or costly logistics tail; there is no requirement to physically deploy personnel and hardware.

✪ **Continuity of Operations:** Each Air Force DGS has cyber redundancy. The degradation of one or more core sites will not negatively affect the presentation of Air Force DCGS PED capability to the CCDR or the JFC. For example, imagery exploitation can be transferred from a Virginia site to a California site instantly, without moving personnel.

ISR Liaisons at Key Joint and Coalition Operational Hubs

ISR LNOs support AOCs and other organizations conducting major global integrated ISR operations. ISR LNOs may be integrated with other components from the operational level down to the tactical level if necessary. ISR LNOs provide recommendations on how to best integrate and synchronize DCGS and other ISR capabilities into theater operations. They provide expertise on ISR operations and may act as a conduit for ISR requirements between ground commanders, intelligence staffs, AOC ISRD analysts, and the DCGS proper. Additionally, ISR LNOs increase situational awareness for ISR crews regarding the details of current operations in which they will participate.

Distributed Common Ground System Analysis and Reporting Teams (DART)

The DART provides the capability for the DGS to focus regionally. DARTs assigned to each active-duty DGS specialize in one or more geographic regions. They provide DCGS crews with situational awareness on the targets, operations, and requirements that they will execute during the course of their mission.

The DARTs provide detailed, precise regional analysis that fully leverages all source intelligence to provide unprecedented insight into theater activities and aids in shaping the battlespace to our advantage. "While we [the Air Force ISR enterprise] seek to have DCGS crews cover targets in their global integrated ISR group's area of operation for target continuity, it is not uncommon to have the DART working issues for its respective area while their collocated crews execute missions for one or more areas."[10]

DARTs in Action

DGS–4 DART, in communication with a forward deployed analytical team that was collocated with an allied partner, received a tip from coalition collection that a terrorist cell was preparing to take action against blue forces. The DART knew their DGS crews would be executing missions in that area later that day and also knew a fellow Air National Guard DGS site was presently operating there. Via chat and other communications means, the DART analyst pushed the intelligence tip to the respective DGS crews as well as the Combined Air Operations Center (CAOC) that was tasking these missions. The Predator was subsequently redirected to the suspected terrorist assembly area where unusual activity was observed. As this was reported back to the ground elements, planning was under way to conduct operations against the terrorists. After operations were completed, the CAOC passed ad hoc requests to the DGS–4 crew to analyze U–2 imagery for battle damage assessment. DGS–4 imagery analysts were able to provide an immediate assessment and confirmation.

---

[10] "Global Distributed ISR operations—The Changing Face of Warfare", David A. Deptula & James R. Marr—JFQ, Issue 54 3d Quarter 2009.

DCGS Crews

Perhaps the most enduring aspect of the DCGS architecture is the exploitation crew. Exploitation crews around the globe interpret collected data from a variety of air and space platforms (e.g., U–2, RQ–4, MQ–1, and MQ–9) and turn it into usable intelligence. Tailored crews are assembled based on the type of platform and the nature of the mission. Within each crew, a C2 element ensures accomplishment of mission tasks, while an analytical team works through individual exploitation assignments. Many of these crews are not part of an AETF which means that they do not turn over every six months. This allows for DCGS crews to maintain continuity and expertise for the duration of an operation.

C2 of PED/Wing Operations Center

The 480th WOC coordinates and manages worldwide Air Force DCGS operations. The 480th WOC mission is to ensure the Air Force DCGS weapons system is synchronized to meet warfighter requirements around the globe. This team understands the joint operational requirements for DCGS as well as the status of crews on a global scale. To facilitate Air Force DCGS operations, the 480th WOC produces a daily PED tasking order. The PED tasking order is a sliding 3-day schedule assigning DCGS crews around the globe to planned ISR missions. While the tasking order serves as the foundation for mission accomplishment, it is the WOC's agility which makes it such a powerful element in distributed operations. As global crises emerge, the WOC is able to react instantly to related combatant command and air component operational requirements. In addition, DPOC expertise in managing the global Air Force DCGS communications architecture promotes flexibility if any portion of the enterprise suffers degradation or an outage.

GLOBAL INTEGRATED ISR AND HOMELAND OPERATIONS

Global integrated ISR homeland operations are distinguished from other global integrated ISR operations in that specific legal authorities/restrictions are involved which limit the role of the military. Examples of these legal restrictions include Executive Order (EO) 12333 (Intelligence Oversight), Title 10, Title 32, Title 50 authorities, and the Posse Comitatus Act of 1878.

Air Force global integrated ISR operations are capable of confronting the external and internal threat but must do so through a clear delineation of responsibility and authority. The Air Force's Total Force effort, with its strong global integrated ISR operations elements (DCGS units, ISR collection platforms), facilitates the separation of global integrated ISR operations in support of Homeland Operations and that of non-continental United States (CONUS) focused global integrated ISR operations. Depending upon the nature of their designated legal authorities, the ANG (via Title 32, USC) is authorized and can legitimately work external or internal ISR operations.

Incident Awareness and Assessments (IAA): IAA is similar to ISR. However, ISR is conducted outside the United States over foreign territory or within the United States during Homeland Defense events, while IAA is conducted within the United States for civil support operations. The change in name from ISR to IAA is necessary to make it clear that DOD does not collect intelligence on US persons. IAA operations focus on providing timely and usable information to all levels of command and to local, tribal, state, and federal leaders in order to save lives, reduce human suffering, and protect property.

Legal Authorities for Homeland Operations

Natural or man-made disasters and special events can temporarily overwhelm local, tribal, state, and non-military federal responders. The DOD has a long history of supporting civil authorities in the wake of catastrophic events. When directed by the President or the SecDef, United States Northern Command (USNORTHCOM) and service components respond to the requests of civil authorities. The Joint Strategic Capabilities Plan 2008 (JSCP) directs the Commander, United States Northern Command (CDRUSNORTHCOM) to prepare a plan to support the employment of Title 10 DOD forces providing civil support in accordance with the National Response Framework (NRF), applicable federal law, DODDs, and other policy and guidance.

The parameters under which DOD operates are different in the US than they are overseas. Military commanders' requirement for accurate intelligence demands that force protection information and counterintelligence are integrated into domestic support operations.[11] These expectations pose unique issues in the information and intelligence gathering arena. DOD intelligence components are subject to one set of rules referred to as intelligence oversight (EO 12333). DOD personnel not in a position to collect intelligence are subject to a different set of rules governed by DODD 5200.27, *Acquisition of Information Concerning Persons and Organizations Not Affiliated with the Department of Defense.* Therefore, the commander must direct his need for information or intelligence to the right component—the component with the capability and authority to achieve the commander's intent.

USNORTHCOM plans, organizes and executes homeland defense and civil support missions, but has few permanently assigned forces. The command is allocated forces when necessary to execute missions, as ordered by the President and SecDef. USNORTHCOM's civil support mission includes domestic disaster relief operations that occur during natural or man-made disasters (e.g., fires, hurricanes, floods, and earthquakes). Support also includes counterdrug operations and managing the consequences of a terrorist event. The command provides assistance to a Primary Agency when tasked by DOD. Per the Posse Comitatus Act, Title 10 military forces can provide civil support, but cannot become directly involved in law enforcement.[12]

In providing civil support, USNORTHCOM generally operates through established Joint Task Forces subordinate to the command. An emergency must exceed the capabilities of local, state, and federal agencies before USNORTHCOM

---

[11] JP 3-28, *Civil Support*
[12] 1 AF DSCA *Air Capabilities Handbook* 2009

becomes involved. In most cases, support will be limited, localized and specific. When the scope of the disaster is reduced to the point that the Primary Agency can again assume full control and management without military assistance, USNORTHCOM will execute its exit strategy and redeploy DOD forces.[13]

Title 10 and Title 32 Forces can complicate unity of command which is critical to focused operations. When Title 10 forces are called to assist in a disaster, state governors may be reluctant to relinquish control of state forces to another military organization thereby losing control of priority and timing of the effects they seek to achieve in the area of operations. Likewise, parallel operations within a JOA by uncoordinated forces may cause unsafe and inefficient operations and in some cases, result in operations with opposing objectives and activity. Air Force North seeks unity of effort with state and interagency air capabilities by providing a trained air component headquarters staff and associated capabilities to state joint force headquarters even before Title 10 forces are introduced into the JOA. For additional information on Homeland Defense refer to JP 3-27, *Homeland Defense* and AFDD 3-27, *Homeland Operations.*

COUNTERDRUG OPERATIONS

Air Force global integrated ISR support to counterdrug operations is conducted through AFFOR assigned to joint interagency task forces (JIATFs) and JTFs. United States Southern Command (USSOUTHCOM), United States Pacific Command (USPACOM), and USNORTHCOM oversee regional JIATFs and JTFs for counterdrug operations within their respective AORs. Intelligence directorates within each JIATF and JTF are the focal points for tactical and operational intelligence support for DOD agencies.[14] The global integrated ISR support activities linked with counterdrug operations are Counterdrug Intelligence Preparation for Operations (CDIPO) and Detection and Monitoring (D&M).

CDIPO identifies likely trafficking routes and recommends the efficient allocation of scarce resources to locate, track, and apprehend drug traffickers.

D&M is an important part of the overall drug interdiction process. The goal of D&M is to provide early notification to DOD agencies and enable them to conduct interdictions and searches for contraband. Figure 2.4 depicts DOD assets used for D&M.

---

[13] 1 AF DSCA *Air Capabilities Handbook* 2009
[14] JP 3-07.4 *Joint Counterdrug Operations.*

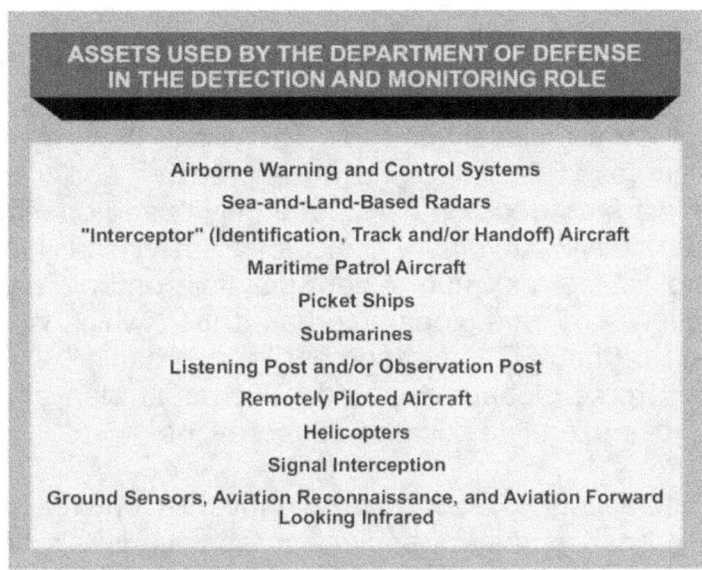

Figure 2.4. DOD Assets used for detection and monitoring

IRREGULAR WARFARE (IW)

Air Force global integrated ISR provides significant capability in IW, but in many ways its role is different from its role in conventional warfare. IW typically has different objectives, intelligence requirements, and targets than conventional warfare. AF global integrated ISR must consider these differences in both planning and executing operations. The objectives in IW are often different than those in conventional warfare. IW typically focuses on gaining the support of the population through utilizing the political, military, and economic means available. IW requires integration of these means at lower echelons to achieve desired effects.

Also, the targets of ISR in IW frequently differ from target sets in conventional warfare. In conventional warfare, ISR is traditionally concerned with discovering the intent, OB, and tactics of governments and armed forces. Additionally in conventional warfare, ISR typically seeks to find the enemy's massed formations which can pose a threat to friendly forces. Irregular adversaries tend to operate in the opposite fashion. They rely on distribution and decentralized operations for security and protection. They are agile and often embedded within local societies. Their tactics are likely to be significantly influenced by the local societies' norms and values. They commonly operate in unrecognizable organizational structures where adversary decisions are not centralized but instead made quickly and communicated laterally across the organization. They adapt to the areas they operate within and from, using available technology to closely link with dispersed operators or cells. They are usually a constellation of fighters organized on the basis of relationships and acquaintances, reputation and fame. Their networks are typically self-forming with new nodes constantly being created and absorbed. Evolving tactics, techniques, procedures, and financial resources enable propaganda and information to flow at increased rates, allowing powerful and nimble coordination.

IW increases the demand for global integrated ISR from lower echelon commanders. This is due in large part to the adversary's ability to live undetected among a population they are closely tied to. The areas they operate within and from generally allow for increased flexibility and an impressive ability to grow support and overcome losses. In warfare, decisions are frequently based on indicators. Because of the dispersed nature of IW, adversary indicators are typically best noted by local personnel. Therefore, to the maximum extent possible organic assets should fill local ISR demand. However, Air Force global integrated ISR, which is typically allocated to the JFACC in support of the JFC, can augment local organic ISR. When augmenting local organic ISR, Air Force global integrated ISR should plan and coordinate closely with the supported forces to enable successful operations.

Further, indicators pop up everywhere, unevenly, unexpectedly, and fleetingly. Global integrated ISR enables joint operations to achieve levels of knowledge, speed, precision, and unity of effort and provides the rapid ability to detect nuanced changes in real time. Based on this, intelligence sharing within the operational environment should include everyone regardless of organizational size, diversity or location. Decision-making should be decentralized as much as possible and cut laterally across the organization.

Due to the highly complex environment of IW, ISR forces should maintain an adaptive, deep, and broad view of ISR operational capabilities. ISR forces need to embrace information collected from a variety of sources with an eye on those sources in the best position to provide or collect information to fill intelligence gaps. Care should be given to validate the credibility of these various sources in order to overcome adversary denial and deception, and information operations.

Although ROE and operational objectives drive operations, analysts should craft their intelligence requirements to account for both available kinetic and non-kinetic capabilities to prevent adverse affects on the population. Analysts should recognize an increased need to make correlations between various development projects and levels of cooperation with local nationals. Additionally, ISR forces should be aware that one of the basic underpinnings of successful IW operations is the capability to train partners to conduct independent operations and participate in coalition operations.

IW conflicts are historically protracted. The IW force should be able to maintain a steady-state rotation policy throughout a decade or more of conflict. Air Force global integrated ISR is well suited to steady-state IW operations because of its capability to leverage distributed operations. Currently, many of the Air Force's global integrated ISR positions are operating from home station. A majority of these positions are filled by permanent party personnel, not by AEF personnel, so as not to split their focus. Therefore, overseas contingency operations require Air Force global integrated ISR forces and capabilities that are as competent and capable in IW as they are in conventional warfare.[15][16]

---

[15] *USAF ISR Strategy: ISR in Irregular Warfare Annex* (2 Jul 2009)

[16] Derived from Gen Stanley McCrystal's *"It Takes a Network"*, Foreign Policy, 2011.

CHAPTER THREE

THE GLOBAL INTEGRATED ISR PROCESS

And, with such capacity for ISR, the difficult guesswork on what hostile forces are around the corner, on the roof, or over the wall is substantially reduced for our ground forces. This capability is absolutely vital at all levels of conflict—strategic, operational, and tactical.

—General Norton A. Schwartz, CSAF

The global integrated ISR cycle comprises a wide spectrum of operations: Planning and Direction, Collection, Processing and Exploitation, Analysis and Production, and Dissemination. The process is not linear or cyclical, but rather represents a network of interrelated, simultaneous operations that can, at any given time, feed and be fed by other operations. The goal of the overall process is actionable operational intelligence—timely, accurate, and complete—that supports decision-making at all levels of war.

INTELLIGENCE DISCIPLINES

Global integrated ISR operations collect data which becomes finished intelligence only when processed, analyzed, and integrated. This data can be collected through a wide variety of means. In order to properly plan and manage global integrated ISR operations it is important to have a basic understanding of the intelligence disciplines. The following is a list (not all-inclusive) of intelligence disciplines relevant to Air Force ISR operations.

Geospatial Intelligence (GEOINT)

GEOINT is the exploitation and analysis of imagery and geospatial information to describe, assess, and visually depict physical features and geographically referenced activities on the Earth. Geospatial intelligence consists of imagery, imagery intelligence, and geospatial information.[17] GEOINT data sources include commercial satellites, government satellites, aircraft, maps, commercial databases, census information, Global Positioning System (GPS) waypoints, or even utility schematics. GEOINT is much more than the sum of its parts. In short, GEOINT can synthesize intelligence and

---

[17] Definition from JP 1-02

data into conceptualized geographic spatial content which can provide commanders key operational intelligence (i.e., best vantage point for shooters, most advantageous entry points, etc.).

Imagery Intelligence (IMINT) involves the collection and analysis of images that are recorded and stored. These images are used for historical comparisons, to locate adversary military forces/facilities and provide the commander insight into the adversary's capabilities. IMINT is also useful in understanding the physical terrain and the human impact in terms of significant cultural sites (governmental structures, historical sites, and schools), agriculture and urban infrastructure, water, electrical grids, etc. IMINT can be broken down into optical images, non-optical images, and full-motion video (FMV).

Optical literal imagery products are visual photos (recorded on film, tape, or electronically) which use visible light to illuminate the objects photographed.

Non-optical non-literal imagery includes infrared, radar, laser-based, multispectral, and hyperspectral imagery. Infrared, radar, and multispectral sensors detect emissions in the non-visual portion of the electromagnetic spectrum. Each specific type of imagery has its advantages and disadvantages. Infrared signatures can be seen with next to no light but are often distorted by aerosols, moisture, and atmospheric gases. Radar imagery can be obtained during day or night and through rain/cloud cover and can detect moving vehicles via moving target indicator systems. Radar imagery requires active illumination by a radio frequency pulse (the reflected return provides an image of the target). Multispectral imagery uses data collected simultaneously from two or more spectral regions or bands of the electromagnetic spectrum—in other words; the same scene is imaged in several spectral bands at the same time by the same sensor. The resulting image contains more detailed information than can be obtained through the use of only one band.

FMV is an imagery capability that can provide continuous moving coverage of a target area in near-real time. Use of full-motion video assists commanders in maintaining situational awareness and identification and tracking of targets, and presents the opportunity for our forces to respond as required. FMV has the potential to provide the unique combination of accuracy and persistence over a contiguous timeline. In addition, many FMV assets have the advantage of employing various PED architectures for simultaneous near-real time dissemination.

Signals Intelligence (SIGINT)

SIGINT is an intelligence discipline comprising either individually or in combination all communications intelligence (COMINT), electronic intelligence (ELINT), and foreign instrumentation signals intelligence (FISINT), however transmitted.[18] Specifically, SIGINT uses intercepted electromagnetic emissions to provide information

---

[18] Definition from JP 2-02

on the capabilities, intentions, formations, and locations of adversary forces. SIGINT also includes collecting, processing and exploiting data from dormant information in cyberspace then analyzes and produces, and disseminates finished intelligence to the warfighter. NSA is the US Government (USG) lead for cryptology, and its mission encompasses both SIGINT and IA activities. NSA maintains a unified organization to conduct SIGINT.

COMINT consists of information derived from intercepting and monitoring the adversary's communications systems. COMINT exploits the adversary's communications, revealing the adversary's intentions.

ELINT consists of information derived from intercepting and monitoring the adversary's *non-communication* emitters. It exploits the adversary's radar, beacons, and other non-communication signals, allowing friendly forces to locate adversary radars and air defense systems over a wide area.

FISINT consists of *technical information* derived from the intercept of electromagnetic emissions (such as telemetry) associated with the testing and operational deployment of foreign air and space, surface, and subsurface systems. FISINT can provide technical details of foreign weapons system development which allows US forces insights into foreign technological advances.

Measurement and Signature Intelligence (MASINT)

MASINT develops intelligence using quantitative and qualitative analysis of data (metric, angle, spatial, wavelength, time dependence, modulation, particulate, plasma, effluent or hydromagnetic). Data is derived from specific technical sensors for the purpose of identifying any distinctive features (either reflected or emitted) associated with the target. Examples of MASINT might include distinctive infrared signatures, electronic signals, or unique sound characteristics collected by ground, airborne, sea, and space-based systems. MASINT can be used to monitor potential adversary technical developments and deployments, as well as emerging WMD threats.

Human Intelligence (HUMINT)

HUMINT is an intelligence collection discipline that uses people in the area of interest (AOI) to identify or provide insight into adversary plans and intentions, research and development, strategy, doctrine, and capabilities. HUMINT can provide several kinds of information. It can provide observations during travel or other events from travelers, refugees, escaped friendly prisoners of war, etc. It can provide data on things about which the subject has specific knowledge, which can be another human subject, or, in the case of defectors and spies, sensitive information to which they had access. Finally, it can provide information on interpersonal relationships and networks of interest. The following are some sources of human-resourced information of global integrated ISR value.

Dedicated HUMINT Collectors can contribute information to the overall global integrated ISR picture and can often amplify, clarify, or verify information collected by other airborne, ground-based, or space-based assets. In many cases, HUMINT, along with counterintelligence activities, are the best and only sources of adversary intentions. The Air Force has an organic HUMINT capability which resides within National Air and Space Intelligence Center (NASIC). However, DOD and other national-level agencies provide operational and strategic HUMINT support. At the strategic level, DIA manages the DOD HUMINT program, coordinates with the intelligence community on collection programs, and responds to standing, ad hoc, time sensitive requirements, and RFIs submitted by CCDRs and theater intelligence centers.

Special Operations Forces conduct special reconnaissance (SR) operations to obtain or verify information about adversary capabilities, intentions, and activities. SR operations complement national and theater global integrated ISR operations by obtaining specific, time-sensitive information of strategic and operational significance.

Aircrew and Ground Personnel conduct human visual surveillance and reconnaissance, which are the most basic and the oldest methods of intelligence gathering. Today, visual surveillance and reconnaissance information comes from a wide range of sources and often simply entails observer reporting and debriefing activities. Observers can include aircrews flying any type of aircraft or SOF conducting assigned missions as described above. Additionally, information gained from onboard aircraft systems such as weapon system video and defensive countermeasure suites can provide invaluable global integrated ISR information during operations. Security forces, explosive ordnance personnel, and other Airmen who operate outside the base perimeter are also sources of information that are of intelligence value.

Document and Media Exploitation is the processing, translation, analysis, and dissemination of collected hard copy documents and electronic media which are under the US Government's physical control and are not publicly available. Exploitation of documents and media often provides valuable insight into operations, financial means, and associations that may not be accessible through other sources and may lead to further targeting efforts.

Open-Source Intelligence (OSINT)

OSINT is the application of intelligence tradecraft to open sources of information, specifically involving the collection, processing (to include foreign language translation), and exploitation/analysis of multiple, independent open sources of information. OSINT sources include commercial scientific and technical databases, symposium proceedings, published strategy and doctrine, think tank publications, patent information, and other open sources available to the general public. A variety of exploitation techniques are practiced, including social network analysis. NASIC is the Air Force lead for OSINT.

ISR RESOURCES

This section describes the types of resources employed to satisfy information requirements through the global integrated ISR process. Understanding the collection resources allows their effective allocation to requirements within the global integrated ISR process. Several of the systems providing input to the global integrated ISR process are not dedicated global integrated ISR resources or systems and ownership may be less important than the actual information satisfying the requirements.

Airborne Systems

Airborne ISR platforms and their associated ground stations generally are among the most responsive assets available. Aircrews can recognize and respond to changing conditions and are able to modify missions while they are in progress. With their ability to fly long distances, airborne platforms can cover a large area with a mix of sensors. Additionally, a majority of these assets have a common data link between aircraft or with ground stations allowing them to distribute large volumes of information in near-real time.

During peacetime, the majority of airborne global integrated ISR missions are accomplished using standoff techniques. A standoff mode is also used during military operations when the threat is too great to allow high value assets to penetrate adversary territory or when over-flight of an area cannot be completed due to political sensitivities. The primary advantage of the standoff mode is that assets are relatively free from adversary surface-to-air and air-to-air attacks. The primary disadvantage is the limited range and depth of sensor coverage.

Remotely Piloted Aircraft (RPA) provide significant advantages over other reconnaissance assets, but commanders must be aware of their limitations. The greatest advantage of these systems is that they normally do not put friendly personnel at risk, can have relatively long loiter times, and are generally less expensive than today's high-value manned assets. RPA limitations vary according to system and operational requirements. RPA technology is maturing rapidly, and platforms can be configured with a broad range of ISR sensors or weapons payloads. Because control authorities and mission priorities can shift between users during multi-role RPA missions, commanders should carefully delineate clear lines of authority. RPA flight paths can be preprogrammed or remotely controlled. Commanders should understand RPA capabilities to support mission requirements as well as their limitations.

Space-based Systems

Space-based global integrated ISR systems are an integral part of military forces and provide support across the ROMO. Space systems provide information to commanders allowing them to quickly assess the situation, develop concepts of operation, and distribute changes to their forces. However, commanders must also be aware of the advantages and limitations of these systems. The prime advantage of space-based systems is their global and wide-area coverage over denied areas where little or no data can be obtained from ground and airborne sources. Other advantages these systems possess include mission longevity and reduced vulnerability to adversary action. While able to provide worldwide coverage, demands on individual space-based systems often exceed their capacity and their associated orbit requirements may limit the ability to meet operational requirements. Space-based ISR is limited by advanced denial and deception techniques. Space-based systems are owned by military, nonmilitary, and national agencies. International cooperation in military space-based ISR systems with Allies and other partners may contribute to US national security objectives by enhancing interoperability, supporting coalition operations, and building partnership capacity.

Military Space-Based Systems provide support to the President, SecDef and the military at all levels. They employ a variety of sensor suites and provide a broad range of capabilities. During peacetime, space systems routinely support training exercises, peacekeeping operations, I&W, disaster and humanitarian relief efforts, counterterrorism, and counternarcotics operations.

As an example, overhead ISR sensors can provide early detection of ballistic missile attack and downlink this information to the appropriate ground stations, thereby allowing early warning. Environmental monitoring systems are crucial to providing an asymmetric war fighting advantage in which we anticipate and exploit the condition of the atmosphere, oceans, soil, and the space environment in order to support friendly military operations and deny those same advantages to adversaries. Awareness of environmental conditions can be the difference between the success or failure of an operation or mission. Space-based global integrated ISR systems can also provide military forces with geographic and detailed terrain information that enhances mission planning capabilities. Additionally, these systems can often cue or be cued by other global integrated ISR systems to watch a specific AOI, enhancing accuracy and reaction times for the users of that information. Finally, space communications support global integrated ISR operations by distributing the products generated from global integrated ISR systems while navigation systems provide a variety of sensors with accurate positioning information.

Non-Military Space-Based Systems can complement military space systems and include civil, commercial, and allied assets. These systems possess a variety of capabilities; however, in some cases their availability may be limited. Often, arrangements are made for military personnel to have access to non-military assets. However, these arrangements are often subject to legal review and take time to activate. In short, space system requirements need to be addressed prior to military operations.

National Satellite Systems are controlled by the US intelligence community and provide support to the President, SecDef and the military at all levels. These resources provide critical data and are responsive to military information needs. These systems are a limited resource. Requirements for these systems need to be worked in advance and detailed justification for their use needs to be provided to the CM.

Ground Based Systems around the world are equipped and tasked to collect information for the intelligence disciplines previously described (e.g., SIGINT, MASINT, etc.). These sites may satisfy national, theater, or local information requirements, or any combination of these.

Air Surveillance and Acquisition Radars, used to control the movement of aircraft, provide a degree of warning and control over air resources within a designated airspace area. Examples of these systems are ground control intercept (GCI), early warning radars, and tracking and acquisition radars. The advantage of these systems is that they provide an additional layer of control and observation that may not be available with other surveillance systems. A disadvantage of these systems is unique sensor limitations which are susceptible to adverse atmospheric conditions. Additionally, air defense sensors are limited to line-of-sight surveillance.

Missile Warning and Space Surveillance offer a significant ground-based global integrated ISR resource, the space surveillance network (SSN) and the ground-based missile warning sensor system. The SSN's purpose is to find, fix, track, and characterize man-made objects in space. An example of an SSN system is the ground-based electro-optical deep space surveillance (GEODSS) system. SSN data is used to determine adversary space OB, adversary satellite over-flight warning, and adversary satellite status. This information is available to theater commanders and provides them early warning and additional information which can be used for denial and deception techniques. Although the primary function of ground-based missile warning sensors is to provide identification and characterization of ballistic missile attacks on the US and its allies, they also contribute to space surveillance. One example of this type of system is the ballistic missile early warning system.

Cyberspace-Based systems

Cyberspace is an important source of ISR information. In addition, cyberspace-based global integrated ISR capabilities are also an integral part of military forces and enable operations across the ROMO. Cyberspace-focused ISR includes digital network analysis and related intelligence support to Air Force cyberspace missions. Specific specialized units provide timely and actionable all-source ISR services and products in support of cyberspace operations. This support is generally characterized within five cyberspace focused ISR areas: current intelligence and reporting; I&W; threat attribution and characterization; IPOE; and computer network exploitation under national intelligence and USCYBERCOM authorities.

MULTI-ROLE AIRCRAFT WITH AN ISR MISSION

Roles and missions for many Air Force assets have expanded beyond what was envisioned in their initial concept of employment. Today it is not unusual to find strike aircraft employed in an ISR role. Whether the aircraft is dedicated to providing global integrated ISR for the entire mission or performing global integrated ISR during part of the mission, the mission objectives, priorities, and guidance for multi-role aircraft employment and the authority to task the weapon system should be clear and developed in advance of mission execution. The JFACC should ensure the following authorities are defined to ensure clear lines of control during multi-role missions:

○ **Aircraft Control:** Organization or individual in authority and technically capable of controlling the aircraft.

○ **Sensor Control:** Organization or individual in authority and technically capable of controlling the aircraft sensor.

○ **Sensor Tasking:** Organization with the authority to direct sensor control and aircraft control to execute global integrated ISR tasking.

When developing collection plans, CMs should keep in mind that available resources are not limited to specific platforms or sensors. For example, ground based radars for GCI, early warning, tracking, and acquisition are used to control the movement of aircraft and provide a degree of warning within designated airspace. The air picture they provide can be exploited for real-time data of potential intelligence value. Additionally, with the increasing sophistication of airborne sensors, aircraft can conduct reconnaissance or surveillance to varying degrees, even if intelligence collection is not their primary mission. Some examples of non-traditional capabilities include F-16CJs collecting SIGINT, F-15Es collecting imagery via their targeting pods, and AC-130s using video capabilities to monitor a particular operation. Understanding how to integrate these capabilities into the collection plan is increasingly important, as traditional intelligence collection-only assets can no longer satisfy all collection requirements. Typically, CMs will not be able to directly task such assets, and will need to coordinate with operations personnel in the strategy, combat plans, or combat operations division of the AOC.

CMs should understand the broad range of PCPAD capabilities and limitations associated with specific aircraft and, based on this knowledge, articulate the intelligence these assets can provide. Depending on the operation, these assets can be called upon to provide a wide range of intelligence collection support, including but not limited to, GEOINT, collecting post-strike intelligence for assessment, and performing ad hoc collection for emerging threats. The availability of these assets may be sporadic and CMs should have knowledge of the current operational environment in order to take advantage of capabilities when they become available.

INTELLIGENCE REQUIREMENTS

Intelligence requirements drive the planning and employment of global integrated ISR operations. The requirements start at the national decision-maker level and are tailored and refined down to the tactical level. Global integrated ISR operations are executed to collect data on these focused requirements. This data is then combined with other data to meet the larger intelligence requirements. Understanding these requirements and where they come from is the linchpin to successful global integrated ISR planning and execution.

Collection Management Authority

CMA is the authority to establish, prioritize, and validate theater collection requirements, establish sensor tasking guidance, and develop theater-wide collection policies.[19] Commanders delegated OPCON over global integrated ISR forces may or may not assume CMA of tasking these global integrated ISR assets as part of the delegation of authority.

CMA usually includes authority to task global integrated ISR GEOINT sensors and lower echelon SIGINT collection systems that have more localized collection capabilities. NSA still retains CMA over the tasking of strategic-capable SIGINT ISR systems. The CCDR may specifically request and subsequently receive temporary SIGINT Operational Tasking Authority (SOTA) over theater-wide capable platforms and sensors. The delegation of SOTA to the CCDR and subsequent delegation of this authority to the JFC ensures the theater has the ability to prioritize requirements and focus SIGINT collection where it is needed to carry out the mission assigned to the command.

Collection Requirements Management (CRM)

CRM is the authoritative development and control of collection, processing, exploitation, and/or reporting requirements that normally result in either the direct tasking of assets over which the collection manager has authority, or the generation of tasking requests to collection management authorities at a higher, lower, or lateral echelon to accomplish the collection mission.[20] CRM and validation of collection requirement requests for a theater often resides at the combatant command level, but may be delegated to a JFC. CRM focuses on the requirements of the customer, is all source oriented, and advocates what information is necessary for collection.

Collection Operations Management (COM)

COM is authoritative direction, scheduling, and control of specific collection operations and associated processing, exploitation, and reporting resources.[21] COM is often delegated to an echelon below the JFC (usually the JFACC), when that echelon has the required expertise in daily collection operations for specific ISR assets. COM is the tasking, scheduling, and control of specific collection, processing and exploitation assets to satisfy joint force requirements that have been validated and prioritized via the CRM process.

Commander's Critical Information Requirements (CCIRs)

Planning and direction of global integrated ISR operations start with the identification of needs for intelligence regarding all aspects of the operational environment. The President and SecDef direct JFCs to engage in adaptive planning for

---

[19] JP 1-02, *DOD Dictionary of Military Terms.*
[20] JP 1-02, *DOD Dictionary of Military Terms.*
[21] JP 1-02, *DOD Dictionary of Military Terms.*

the conduct of operations. The JFC should then provide the CCIRs to the joint staff and components.

CCIRs are information requirements identified by the commander as being critical to facilitating timely decision-making. The two key elements are friendly force information requirements and priority intelligence requirements.[22] There are numerous legal issues associated with global integrated ISR, especially if it could impact US citizens. Global integrated ISR activities in support of CCIRs should be coordinated with the servicing judge advocate to ensure compliance with the law and any existing ROEs.

Priority Intelligence Requirements (PIRs)

In the course of intelligence planning and direction, intelligence planners identify the intelligence required to answer the CCIRs. Those intelligence requirements deemed most important to mission accomplishment are identified as PIRs. PIRs are general statements of intelligence need. Examples of PIRs are as follows: "what is the operational status of the adversary's integrated air defense system?" or "what terrorist groups are active within the AOR/AOI?"

PIRs provide the framework for prioritization of all global integrated ISR operations. PIRs are driven by, and in turn drive, the IPOE process to refine information requirements and support the commander's potential COAs. The designation of intelligence requirements ensures global integrated ISR efforts are focused on critical information needed to support warfighters. Additionally, PIRs drive the development of detailed EEIs.

Essential Elements of Information (EEIs)

EEIs further define the commander's priority intelligence requirements by outlining specific information requirements. An example of an EEI is as follows: "what is the current location of the adversary SA-20 battery?" EEIs are linked to PIRs in order to trace accountability for global integrated ISR operations to commander priorities. As commander direction and guidance evolve, global integrated ISR planners may develop new EEI requirements or modify existing requirements.

PCPAD

The PCPAD process of planning global integrated ISR operations begins once the above requirements have been established, validated, and prioritized. As intelligence collection requirements are aligned with available collection capabilities, the planning process addresses factors such as the availability of ISR assets, platform and sensor capabilities, adversary threats to assets, and timeliness of a global integrated ISR response. These factors, when weighed together, affect how ISR assets are

---

[22] JP 1-02, *DOD Dictionary of Military Terms.*

tasked and employed. In order to make the planning process more efficient, information requesters should clearly articulate their collection requirements and allow the CMs and operations planners to decide the best way to meet the requirements. Global integrated ISR planners at every level should coordinate closely to effectively plan operations. Global integrated ISR planners should thoroughly analyze the combination of the commander's objectives and guidance, potential threats, force capabilities, and global integrated ISR systems availability.

An optimal global integrated ISR strategy should be designed to maximize battlespace awareness. ISR strategy is encapsulated within the JAOP and is synchronized with theater and national architectures and strategies. It provides the foundation for development and validation of intelligence requirements, captures the framework for planning and direction of global integrated ISR operations, and establishes guidance for the operation of all other elements of the global integrated ISR process.

Throughout the intelligence process, refinement of information requirements should continuously evaluate whether or not the intelligence provided will satisfy the needs of planning, employment, and assessment. PCPAD processes are continuously evolving to best support all levels of conflict. Air Force global integrated ISR institutionalizes all-source planning and direction, collection, processing and exploitation, analysis and production, and dissemination by improving the ability to leverage both defense and national intelligence assets. PCPAD provides a systematic approach to ensuring the DOD presents its preeminent ISR forces to joint commanders. In examining intelligence, surveillance, and reconnaissance individually, collectively, and systematically a basic premise is irrefutable: ISR is indivisible. This is because the effects it provides depend upon the synchronization and integration of the intelligence, surveillance, and reconnaissance activities. The data collected depends upon processing and exploitation common to all three activities.

Planning and Direction

Planning and direction is the determination of intelligence requirements, development of appropriate intelligence architecture, preparation of a collection plan, and issuance of orders and requests to information collection agencies.[23] Planning and direction of global integrated ISR activities involves synchronizing and integrating the activities of collection, processing and exploitation, analysis and production, and dissemination resources to meet information requirements of national and military decision-makers at all levels. Precise planning will mitigate and potentially defeat the traditional adversary advantages of surprise, speed, stealth, maneuver and initiative. For example, campaign planners rely on global integrated ISR to provide the intelligence crucial to understanding an adversary's weaknesses and key nodes that can be affected by air, space, land, maritime, cyberspace and information operations. Intelligence analysis helps detect/discover, identify, locate, and describe the vulnerable,

---

[23] JP 1-02, *DOD Dictionary of Military Terms.*

vital elements of an adversary's physical and virtual structure and their COG. In this way Air Force global integrated ISR brings significant strengths to Foreign Internal Defense (FID) and Counterinsurgency (COIN), not the least of which is identifying key areas along the borders and monitoring traffic in coordination with partner nations (PN).

Collection

Collection is the acquisition of information and the provision of this information to processing elements.[24] The collection portion of the intelligence process involves tasking appropriate assets or resources to acquire the data and information required. Collection includes the identification, prioritization, coordination, and positioning of assets or resources in all domains to satisfy intelligence requirements. A unique advantage is that several platforms used for collection provide an opportunity to minimize the US footprint. Global integrated ISR assets can be based outside of the AOI or sequestered on airfields within the AOI that are relatively isolated from the population.

Processing and Exploitation

Processing and exploitation is the conversion of collected information into forms suitable to the production of intelligence.[25] Once the data satisfying the requirements are collected, they undergo processing and exploitation. Through processing and exploitation, the collected raw data is transformed into information that can be readily disseminated, used, transmitted, and exploited by intelligence analysts. Relevant critical information should also be disseminated to the commander and joint force staff to facilitate time-sensitive decision making. Processing and exploitation time varies depending on the characteristics of specific collection assets. For example, some global integrated ISR systems accomplish processing automatically and nearly simultaneous with collection. However, other collection assets, such as HUMINT teams, may require additional time. Processing and exploitation requirements are prioritized and synchronized with the commander's PIRs.

During processing and exploitation, collected data is correlated and converted into a format suitable for analysis and production. Processing remains distinct from analysis and production in that the resulting information receives tier one analysis for time-critical production but has not been subjected to full analytical assessment. Relevant time-sensitive information resulting from this step in the process (especially targeting, personnel recovery, or threat warning information) should be immediately disseminated through intelligence broadcasts, secure information workspace or internet relay chat channels, imagery product libraries (IPLs), intelligence databases, or message reporting.

---

[24] JP 1-02, *DOD Dictionary of Military Terms.*
[25] JP 1-02, *DOD Dictionary of Military Terms.*

Analysis and Production

Analysis and production is the conversion of processed information into intelligence through the integration, evaluation, analysis, and interpretation of all source data and the preparation of intelligence products in support of known or anticipated user requirements.[26] Integrated multi-domain ISR-generated data can provide understanding of demographics, culture, physical terrain, centers of gravity, and financial, social, and political infrastructures. Global integrated ISR must fuse all source intelligence data and rapidly disseminate finished, timely, accurate and actionable intelligence to consumers in order to facilitate command decisions and rapid response options.

Analysis and production are accomplished through a structured series of actions which, usually occurring sequentially, may also take place concurrently. These actions include the integration, evaluation, analysis, and interpretation of information in response to known or anticipated intelligence production requirements.

✪ **Integration.** Information from single or multiple sources is received, collated, and entered into appropriate databases by the analysis and production elements of intelligence community organizations, the theater JIOCs or subordinate joint force elements like the ISRD. Information is integrated and grouped with related pieces of data according to predetermined criteria to facilitate the evaluation of newly received information.

✪ **Evaluation.** Each new item of information is evaluated by the appropriate analysis and production element with respect to the reliability of the source and the credibility of the information. The reliability of the source and the credibility of the information should be assessed independently of each other to avoid bias.

✪ **Analysis.** During analysis, assessments are made by comparing integrated and evaluated information with known facts and predetermined assumptions. These assessments are combined and assessed to discern patterns, links or recognized events. Analysis can also result in identification of opportunities or knowledge gaps that drive future collection. Examples of analytical activities include pattern of life analysis, spatial/temporal analysis, network analysis, trend analysis, forensic-based analysis.

✪ **Interpretation.** Interpretation is an inductive process in which the information is judged in relation to existing information and intelligence. This process involves the identification of new activity and a postulation regarding the significance of that activity.

---

[26] JP 1-02, *DOD Dictionary of Military Terms.*

These actions enable intelligence fusion. Fusion is the process of examining all sources of intelligence and information to derive a complete assessment of activity.[27] To promote fusion, analysts should work in collaborative environments which provide access to recognized, and often geographically separated, subject matter experts. Through collaboration, intelligence analysts are able to share information, discuss opinions, debate hypotheses, and identify or resolve analytic disagreements. Advances in network capabilities greatly enhance analysts' ability to share, compare, and assess information. As databases grow in volume and complexity, potentially vital pieces of information may become increasingly difficult for analysts to find and retrieve. In order to overcome this limitation, virtual knowledge bases have been designed to serve as integrated repositories of multiple databases as well as reference documents and open-source material.

Dissemination

Dissemination is the delivery of intelligence to users in a suitable form and the application of the intelligence to appropriate missions, tasks, and functions.[28] Dissemination of global integrated ISR provides the end user information required for application in a timely manner. Dissemination can take a variety of forms (i.e., electronic transmission, hardcopy annotated imagery/maps, direct threat warnings, oral and written reports, briefings, or via various servers allowing structured discovery and retrieval). Most importantly, the dissemination process requires continuous management. Without effective management, communications paths can become saturated by information being retransmitted by many intermediate collection agencies, resulting in "circular reporting." Advances in cyber capabilities or technology also improve dissemination by reducing information-to-production timeline for delivering global integrated ISR products. Likewise, some collection systems are capable of disseminating collected information to requesters on a real- or near real-time basis, vastly increasing their responsiveness. With this consideration in mind, it is sometimes better to get the consumer data immediately rather than processed knowledge too late.

Additionally, global integrated ISR planning should include local procedures for rapidly coordinating with Public Affairs for public release of select intelligence. This expanding collection capability makes secure network connectivity all the more important because real-time planning and targeting systems depend on tailored intelligence information. The integration of intelligence and operations on a continuous basis allows commanders and all operational planners access to the most current information available, thereby optimizing intelligence support to operation planning, preparation, execution, and assessment functions.

---

[27] JP 1-02, *DOD Dictionary of Military and Associated Terms.*
[28] JP 1-02, *DOD Dictionary of Military and Associated Terms.*

GLOBAL INTEGRATED ISR METHODOLOGIES/PRODUCTS

A number of global integrated ISR methodologies and products provide predictive analysis, near-real time and real-time threat, target and friendly forces status to the JFACC, operational units, and even individual operators. Air Force global integrated ISR systems contribute to the building of a COP for all domains- land, air, maritime, space and cyberspace. At the most basic level, situational awareness is the goal of global integrated ISR operations. Situational awareness is provided at a number of levels. For example, it could mean passing direct threat warning information to a pilot in near-real time, providing a CCDR with a comprehensive picture of the AOR's operational environment, or supporting building partnership activities. This threat picture can be conveyed to tactical users via audio, video, or data links.

Additionally, global integrated ISR products can be tailored via formal reporting methods, informal or formal briefings, background papers, annotated imagery, graphic or video presentations, dynamic databases, and near-real time displays. Below are some of the methodologies and products that contribute to situational awareness (available at all levels) and highlight the global integrated ISR contributions of the Air Force.

Indications and Warning

Global integrated ISR is vital for I&W functions. Global integrated ISR provides timely and continuous near-real time information to assess potential threats to the US and its allies. Specifically, a critical mission of the I&W function is to provide strategic warning of possible ballistic missile attack. The space-based infrared system, which detects missile launches, is one example of global integrated ISR contributions. I&W products are derived from a worldwide system that analyzes and integrates information to assess the probability of hostile actions, and provides sufficient warning to preempt or counter their outcome. I&W systems rely on tip-offs from sources at all levels. An integrated and responsive intelligence architecture should be established to satisfy national, strategic, and theater requirements. The focus of I&W products varies at each echelon and is most specific at the operational and tactical levels. In general, I&W products focus on the following:

✪ Emerging crisis situations and foreign government responses to them.

✪ A potential adversary's politico-military intentions, past behaviors, motivations, and doctrine.

✪ Significant political, economic, or social situations that could lead to crisis-triggering events in both friendly and adversary states.

✪ Changes in adversary force dispositions, military activities, and mobilization status.

✪ Adversary information operations capabilities in the region.

○ Key civil or bureaucratic activities that suggest follow-on military activity.

○ Status of other military forces in the AOR or operations.

Current Intelligence

Current intelligence is the art of producing and fusing global integrated ISR products on the current situation in a particular area or on activities of specific groups. This type of intelligence is similar to I&W in that both depend upon continuous monitoring of world events and specific activities in an AOR. Information required to produce current intelligence products includes, but is not limited to, the following:

○ Adversary intentions, capabilities, and will to use military force.

○ Potential adversaries' centers of gravity, operational plans, and vulnerabilities.

○ Geographic, environmental, and social analysis of the operational area.

○ Significant military and political events.

○ Status of strategic transportation nodes (major airfields, seaports, and cyber capabilities architecture).

○ Analysis of WMD threats against the US and its allies and friends.

Current Intelligence and General Military Intelligence (GMI) form a symbiotic relationship. The information gained during development of current intelligence forms the basis for the GMI effort and other analytical products. Conversely, GMI provides the threat backbone through OB, tactics, technology, etc., for producing accurate and meaningful current intelligence.

General Military Intelligence (GMI)

GMI is "intelligence concerning the (1) military capabilities of foreign countries or organizations or (2) topics affecting potential US or multinational military operations, relating to the following subjects: armed forces capabilities, including OB, organization, training, tactics, doctrine, strategy, and other factors bearing on military strength and effectiveness; area and terrain intelligence, including urban areas, coasts and landing beaches, and meteorological, oceanographic, and geological intelligence; transportation in all modes; military materiel production and support industries; military and civilian communications systems; military economics, including foreign military assistance; insurgency and terrorism; military-political-sociological intelligence; location, identification, and description of military-related installations; government control; escape and evasion; and threats and forecasts."[29]

---

[29] JP 1-02, *DOD Dictionary of Military Terms.*

Current intelligence and GMI efforts are synergistic. GMI produces information concerning OB, political, economic, and social aspects of foreign countries. Additional GMI products may include reports on the organization, operations, and capabilities of selected foreign military forces or groups. The following are examples of GMI products:

✪ **Military-related Infrastructure Assessments**. These assessments provide detailed indicators of an opposing force's capabilities and vulnerabilities, including its warfighting sustainability. Examples include assessments on adversary C2 systems, defense industries, energy production and distribution networks, transportation systems and cyber capabilities.

✪ **Military Capabilities Assessments.** Determining the adversary's potential military capability includes identifying forces, readiness levels, evaluating vulnerabilities, and assessing adversary abilities to employ military force to counter friendly force objectives.

Scientific and Technical Intelligence (S&TI)

S&TI products focus on foreign scientific and technical developments which have warfare potential. Examples of S&TI products include weapon system characteristics, capabilities, vulnerabilities, limitations, and effectiveness as well as research and development and related manufacturing information. Global integrated ISR generated S&TI products play a vital role in the acquisition process by allowing the acquisition community to procure systems or upgrade existing ones to meet current, developing, and potential future threats.

Target Intelligence

Required global integrated ISR products, such as target imagery, should be immediately available to support the ATO and mission planning cycle. Global integrated ISR operations play a prominent role in the targeting cycle by detecting, locating, and identifying targets, as well as supporting mission planning and assessment. Additionally, successful employment of precision munitions against mobile targets often requires near-real time targeting information.

Detection is an ongoing process which uses global integrated ISR assets to identify potential targets or identify changes to existing targets. Multiple global integrated ISR missions may be required to provide the level of detail necessary to support the precision engagement of specific high-value targets.

Target intelligence products also include current imagery, target system analyses, and geospatial information. As mentioned previously, advances in technology have increased the capability for intelligence to be passed directly to the cockpit ("sensor-to-shooter"). For example, RC-135 RIVET JOINT can provide threat information to aircraft performing both counterair and counterland missions. Target imagery can also be provided directly to the same aircraft.

CONCLUSION

ISR is a rapidly changing mission set that is heavily reliant on technology and human analytical capabilities. Recent conflicts have generated increased expectations from the warfighter to get actionable intelligence faster and more fused. The Air Force undertook a four year ISR transformation addressing ISR organization, personnel, and capabilities to more effectively conduct operations. This transformation was predicated on ISR operations being globally integrated to meet increased expectation. The Air Force leads the way in integrating ISR in, to, and through all domains with capabilities using distributed operations to provide the commander with actionable intelligence as expeditiously as possible. Distributed ISR operations allow for global integrated ISR capabilities to be presented with a reduced forward footprint. This puts fewer Airmen in harm's way without sacrificing operational capability. The Air Force's primary system for enabling distributed operations is the Air Force DCGS, a network-centric, global enterprise. The strength of the DCGS is that each DGS is networked and linked. Therefore, if one DGS workload exceeds capacity another DGS can assist in real time, allowing effective and efficient, uninterrupted mission execution. As global integrated ISR operations mature and capabilities improve the demand for ISR will increase. Due to finite number of ISR capabilities, especially platforms, prioritization and dynamic retasking considerations will be magnified. The Air Force is preparing to meet these challenges and lead the way in integrating ISR missions. The goal is to maximize their utility to the warfighter by collaborating with other key Air Force, Joint, other government agencies, and Coalition partners to provide accurate, timely, and objective ISR to support decision making.

AT THE VERY HEART OF WARFARE LIES DOCTRINE...

REFERENCES

Air Force

All Air Force personnel should be familiar with the full breadth of Air Force operations. As a beginning, they should read the entire series of the basic and operational doctrine documents. Air Force Doctrine Documents are available online at: http://www.e-publishing.af.mil/

Joint
Joint publications are available online at:
http://www.dtic.mil/doctrine/new_pubs/jointpub.htm

JP 1, *Doctrine for the Armed Forces of the United States*
JP 1-02, *Department of Defense Dictionary of Military and Associated Terms*
JP 2-0, *Joint Intelligence*
JP 2-01, *Joint and National Intelligence Support to Military Operations*
JP 2-01.3, *Joint Intelligence Preparation of the Operational Environment*
JP 2-03, *Geospatial Intelligence Support to Joint Operations*
JP 3-0, *Joint Operations*
JP 3-01, *Countering Air and Missile Threats*
JP 3-03, *Joint Interdiction*
JP 3-05, *Doctrine for Joint Special Operations*
JP 3-06, *Joint Urban Operations*
JP 3-07.2, *Antiterrorism*
JP 3-07.4, *Joint Counterdrug Operations*
JP 3-10, *Joint Security Operations in Theater*
JP 3-13, *Information Operations*
JP 3-13.1, *Electronic Warfare*
JP 3-13.2, *Psychological Operations*
JP 3-13.4, *Military Deception*
JP 3-14, *Space Operations*
JP 3-16, *Multinational Operations*
JP 3-22, *Foreign Internal Defense*
JP 3-24, *Counterinsurgency Operations*
JP 3-26, *Counterterrorism*
JP 3-27, *Homeland Defense*
JP 3-28, *Civil Support*
JP 3-40, *Combating Weapons of Mass Destruction*
JP 3-60, *Joint Targeting*
JP 5-0, *Joint Operation Planning*
JP 6-0, *Joint Communications System*

GLOSSARY

Abbreviations and Acronyms

AADC	area air defense commander
ACA	airspace control authority
ADCON	administrative control
AEF	Air and Space Expeditionary Force
AETF	Air Expeditionary Task Force
AFDD	Air Force doctrine document
AFFOR	Air Force forces
AFISRA	Air Force Intelligence, Surveillance and Reconnaissance Agency
AFSOC	Air Force Special Operations Command
AFSOF	Air Force Special Operations Forces
AFTTP	Air Force tactics, techniques, and procedures
AMD	air mobility division
ANG	Air National Guard
AOC	air operations center
AOD	air operations directive
AOI	area of interest
AOR	area of responsibility
ATO	air tasking order
BDA	battle damage assessment
C2	command and control
CA	combat assessment
CAOC	Combined Air Operations Center
CCDR	combatant commander
CCIR	commander's critical information requirement
CDIPO	counterdrug intelligence preparation for operations
CDRUSNORTHCOM	Commander, United States Northern Command
CM	collection management
CMA	collection management authority
C-MAJCOM	Component-Major Command
C-NAF	Component-Numbered Air Force
COA	course of action
COCOM	combatant command (command authority)
COG	center of gravity
COIN	Counterinsurgency
COM	collection operations management
COMAFFOR	commander, Air Force forces
COMINT	communications intelligence
CONPLAN	concept plans
CONUS	Continental United States
COP	common operational picture

CRM	collection requirements management
D&M	detection and monitoring
DART	DCGS Analysis and Reporting Team
DCGS	distributed common ground system
DCS	Deputy Chief of Staff
DGS	distributed ground station
DIA	Defense Intelligence Agency
DOD	Department of Defense
DODD	Department of Defense Directive
DPOC	Air Force Distributed Common Ground System Processing, Exploitation, and Dissemination Operations Center
EEI	essential elements of information
ELINT	electronic intelligence
FDO	Foreign Disclosure Officer
FID	foreign internal defense
FISINT	foreign instrumentation signals intelligence
FMV	full-motion video
GCI	ground control intercept
GEODSS	ground-based electro-optical deep space surveillance
GEOINT	geospatial intelligence
GFM	Global Force Management
GMI	general military intelligence
GPS	Global Positioning System
HAF	Headquarters Air Force
HUMINT	human intelligence
I&W	indications and warning
IA	Information assurance
IAA	incident awareness and assessment
IC	Intelligence Community
IMINT	imagery intelligence
IPB	intelligence preparation of the battlespace
IPL	imagery product library
IPOE	intelligence preparation of the operational environment
ISR	intelligence, surveillance, and reconnaissance
ISRD	intelligence, surveillance, and reconnaissance division
J2	intelligence directorate on a joint staff
J3	operations directorate on a joint staff
JAOC	joint air operations center
JAOP	joint air operations plan
JCS	Joint Chiefs of Staff
JET	joint expeditionary taskings
JFACC	joint force air and space component commander

JFC	joint force commander
JIATF	joint interagency task force
JIOC	joint intelligence operations center
JIPCL	joint integrated prioritized collection list
JIPTL	joint integrated prioritized target list
JOA	joint operational area
JOPP	joint operation planning process
JSCP	Joint Strategic Capabilities Plan
JTF	joint task force
LNO	liaison officer
LOAC	Law of Armed Conflict
MAAP	Master Air Attack Plan
MASINT	measurement and signature intelligence
MISREP	mission report
MOE	measure of effectiveness
NASIC	National Air and Space Intelligence Center
NATO	North Atlantic Treaty Organization
NDP	National Disclosure Policy
NDS	National Defense Strategy
NGA	National Geospatial-Intelligence Agency
NMS	National Military Strategy
NRF	National Response Framework
NRO	National Reconnaissance Office
NSA	National Security Agency
NSC	National Security Council
NSS	National Security Strategy
OA	operational area
OB	order of battle
OPCON	operational control
OPE	operational preparation of the environment
OPLAN	operation plan
OPORD	operation orders
OSINT	open-source intelligence
PCPAD	planning and direction, collection, processing and exploitation, analysis and production, and dissemination
PED	processing, exploitation and dissemination
PIR	priority intelligence requirements
PLANORD	planning order
PN	partner nation
RFF	request for forces
RFI	request for information
ROE	rules of engagement
ROMO	range of military operations
RPA	remotely piloted aircraft
RSO	remote split operations

RSTA	reconnaissance, surveillance, and target acquisition
S&TI	scientific and technical intelligence
SCA	space coordinating authority
SCF	service core function
SecDef	Secretary of Defense
SIDO	Senior Intelligence Duty Officer
SIGINT	signals intelligence
SIO	senior intelligence officer
SOF	special operations forces
SOTA	signals intelligence operational tasking authority
SR	special reconnaissance
SSN	space surveillance network
STANAG	standardization agreement
TACON	tactical control
TACS	theater air control system
TSA	target system analysis
USC	United States Code
USG	United States Government
USNORTHCOM	United States Northern Command
USPACOM	United States Pacific Command
USSOCOM	United States Special Operations Command
USSOUTHCOM	United States Southern Command
WMD	weapons of mass destruction
WOC	wing operations center

Definitions

administrative control. Direction or exercise of authority over subordinate or other organizations in respect to administration and support, including organization of Service forces, control of resources and equipment, personnel management, unit logistics, individual and unit training, readiness, mobilization, demobilization, discipline, and other matters not included in the operational missions of the subordinate or other organizations. (JP 1-02)

air operations center. The senior agency of the Air Force component commander that provides command and control of Air Force air and space operations and coordinates with other components and Services. (JP 1-02)

air tasking order. A method used to task and disseminate to components, subordinate units, and command and control agencies projected sorties, capabilities and/or forces to targets and specific missions. Normally provides specific instructions to include call signs, targets, controlling agencies, etc., as well as general instructions. (JP 1-02)

all-source intelligence. 1. Intelligence products and/or organizations and activities that incorporate all sources of information, most frequently including human resources intelligence, imagery intelligence, measurement and signature intelligence, signals intelligence, and open-source data in the production of finished intelligence. 2. In intelligence collection, a phrase that indicates that in the satisfaction of intelligence requirements, all collection, processing, exploitation, and reporting systems and resources are identified for possible use and those most capable are tasked. (JP 1-02)

analysis and production. In intelligence usage, the conversion of processed information into intelligence through the integration, evaluation, analysis, and interpretation of all source data and the preparation of intelligence products in support of known or anticipated user requirements. (JP 1-02)

battle damage assessment. The estimate of damage resulting from the application of lethal or nonlethal military force. Battle damage assessment is composed of physical damage assessment, functional damage assessment, and target system assessment. (JP 1-02)

collection. In intelligence usage, the acquisition of information and the provision of this information to processing elements. (JP 1-02)

collection asset. A collection system, platform, or capability that is supporting, assigned, or attached to a particular commander. See also capability, collection. (JP 1-02)

collection management. In intelligence usage, the process of converting intelligence requirements into collection requirements, establishing priorities, tasking or coordinating with appropriate collection sources or agencies, monitoring results, and retasking, as required. (JP 1-02)

collection management authority. Within the Department of Defense, collection management authority constitutes the authority to establish, prioritize, and validate theater collection requirements, establish sensor tasking guidance, and develop theater-wide collection policies. (JP 1-02)

collection manager. An individual with responsibility for the timely and efficient tasking of organic collection resources and the development of requirements for theater and national assets that could satisfy specific information needs in support of the mission. (JP 1-02)

collection operations management. The authoritative direction, scheduling, and control of specific collection operations and associated processing, exploitation, and reporting resources. (JP 1-02)

collection plan. A plan for collecting information from all available sources to meet intelligence requirements and for transforming those requirements into orders and requests to appropriate agencies. (JP 1-02)

collection requirement. 1. An intelligence need considered in the allocation of intelligence resources. Within the Department of Defense, these collection requirements fulfill the essential elements of information and other intelligence needs of a commander, or an agency. 2. An established intelligence need, validated against the appropriate allocation of intelligence resources (as a requirement) to fulfill the essential elements of information and other intelligence needs of an intelligence consumer. (JP 1-02)

collections requirement management. The authoritative development and control of collection, processing, exploitation, and/or reporting requirements that normally result in either the direct tasking of assets over which the collection manager has authority, or the generation of tasking requests to collection management authorities at a higher, lower, or lateral echelon to accomplish the collection mission. (JP 1-02)

collection resource. A collection system, platform, or capability that is not assigned or attached to a specific unit or echelon which must be requested and coordinated through the chain of command. (JP 1-02)

combat assessment. The determination of the overall effectiveness of force employment during military operations. Combat assessment is composed of three major components: (a) battle damage assessment; (b) munitions effectiveness assessment; and (c) reattack recommendation. (JP 1-02)

combatant command (command authority). Nontransferable command authority established by title 10 ("Armed Forces"), United States Code, section 164, exercised only by commanders of unified or specified combatant commands unless otherwise directed by the President or the Secretary of Defense. Combatant command (command authority) cannot be delegated and is the authority of a combatant commander to perform those functions of command over assigned forces involving organizing and employing commands and forces, assigning tasks, designating objectives, and giving authoritative direction over all aspects of military operations, joint training, and logistics necessary to accomplish the missions assigned to the command. Combatant command (command authority) should be exercised through the commanders of subordinate organizations. Normally this authority is exercised through subordinate joint force commanders and Service and/or functional component commanders. Combatant command (command authority) provides full authority to organize and employ commands and forces as the combatant commander considers necessary to accomplish assigned missions. Operational control is inherent in combatant command (command authority). (JP 1-02)

command and control. The exercise of authority and direction by a properly designated commander over assigned and attached forces in the accomplishment of the mission. Command and control functions are performed through an arrangement of personnel, equipment, communications, facilities, and procedures employed by a commander in planning, directing, coordinating, and controlling forces and operations in the accomplishment of the mission. (JP 1-02)

commander's critical information requirements. An information requirement identified by the commander as being critical to facilitating timely decision-making. The two key elements are friendly force information requirements and priority intelligence requirements. (JP 1-02)

common operational picture. A single identical display of relevant information shared by more than one command. A common operational picture facilitates collaborative planning and assists all echelons to achieve situational awareness. (JP 1-02)

communications intelligence. Technical information and intelligence derived from foreign communications by other than the intended recipients. (JP 1-02)

counterintelligence. Information gathered and activities conducted to protect against espionage, other intelligence activities, sabotage, or assassinations conducted by or on behalf of foreign governments or elements thereof, foreign organizations, or foreign persons, or international terrorist activities. (JP 1-02)

critical information. Specific facts about friendly intentions, capabilities, and activities vitally needed by adversaries for them to plan and act effectively so as to guarantee failure or unacceptable consequences for friendly mission accomplishment. (JP 1-02)

current intelligence. One of two categories of descriptive intelligence that is concerned with describing the existing situation. (JP 1-02)

cyberspace. A global domain within the information environment consisting of the interdependent network of information technology infrastructures, including the Internet, telecommunications networks, computer systems, and embedded processors and controllers. (JP 1-02)

cyberspace operations. The employment of cyber capabilities where the primary purpose is to achieve objectives in or through cyberspace. Such operations include computer network operations and activities to operate and defend the Global Information Grid. (JP 1-02)

deception. Those measures designed to mislead the enemy by manipulation, distortion, or falsification of evidence to induce the enemy to react in a manner prejudicial to the enemy's interests. (JP 1-02)

distributed operations. The process of conducting operations from independent or interdependent nodes in a teaming manner. Some operational planning or decision-making may occur from outside the joint area of operations. The goal of a distributed operation is to support the operational commander in the field; it is not a method of command from the rear. (AFDD 6-0)

electronic intelligence. Technical and geolocation intelligence derived from foreign noncommunications electromagnetic radiations emanating from other than nuclear detonations or radioactive sources. (JP 1-02)

essential elements of information. The most critical information requirements regarding the adversary and the environment needed by the commander by a particular time to relate with other available information and intelligence in order to assist in reaching a logical decision. (JP 1-02)

estimate. 1. An analysis of a foreign situation, development, or trend that identifies its major elements, interprets the significance, and appraises the future possibilities and the prospective results of the various actions that might be taken. 2. An appraisal of the capabilities, vulnerabilities, and potential courses of action of a foreign nation or combination of nations in consequence of a specific national plan, policy, decision, or contemplated course of action. 3. An analysis of an actual or contemplated clandestine operation in relation to the situation in which it is or would be conducted in order to identify and appraise such factors as available as well as needed assets and potential obstacles, accomplishments, and consequences. (JP 1-02)

evaluation and feedback. In intelligence usage, continuous assessment of intelligence operations throughout the intelligence process to ensure that the commander's intelligence requirements are being met. (JP 1-02)

exploitation. 1. Taking full advantage of success in military operations, following up initial gains, and making permanent the temporary effects already achieved. 2. Taking full advantage of any information that has come to hand for tactical, operational, or strategic purposes. 3. An offensive operation that usually follows a successful attack and is designed to disorganize the enemy in depth. (JP 1-02)

foreign instrumentation signals intelligence. Technical information and intelligence derived from the intercept of foreign electromagnetic emissions associated with the testing and operational deployment of non-US aerospace, surface, and subsurface systems. Foreign instrumentation signals intelligence is a subcategory of signals intelligence. Foreign instrumentation signals include but are not limited to telemetry, beaconry, electronic interrogators, and video data links. (JP 1-02)

fusion. In intelligence usage, the process of examining all sources of intelligence and information to derive a complete assessment of activity. (JP 1-02)

general military intelligence. Intelligence concerning the (1) military capabilities of foreign countries or organizations or (2) topics affecting potential US or multinational military operations, relating to the following subjects: armed forces capabilities, including order of battle, organization, training, tactics, doctrine, strategy, and other factors bearing on military strength and effectiveness; area and terrain intelligence, including urban areas, coasts and landing beaches, and meteorological, oceanographic, and geological intelligence; transportation in all modes; military materiel production and support industries; military and civilian communications systems; military economics, including foreign military assistance; insurgency and terrorism; military-political-sociological intelligence; location, identification, and description of military-related installations; government control; escape and evasion; and threats and forecasts. (Excludes scientific and technical intelligence.) (JP 1-02)

geospatial intelligence. The exploitation and analysis of imagery and geospatial information to describe, assess, and visually depict physical features and geographically referenced activities on the Earth. Geospatial intelligence consists of imagery, imagery intelligence, and geospatial information. (JP 1-02)

human intelligence. A category of intelligence derived from information collected and provided by human sources. (JP 1-02)

imagery. A likeness or presentation of any natural or man-made feature or related object or activity, and the positional data acquired at the same time the likeness or representation was acquired, including: products produced by space-based national intelligence reconnaissance systems; and likeness and presentations produced by satellites, airborne platforms, unmanned aerial vehicles, or other similar means (except that such term does not include handheld or clandestine photography taken by or on behalf of human intelligence collection organizations). (JP 1-02)

indications and warning. Those intelligence activities intended to detect and report time-sensitive intelligence information on foreign developments that could involve a threat to the United States or allied and/or coalition military, political, or economic interests or to US citizens abroad. It includes forewarning of hostile actions or intentions against the United States, its activities, overseas forces, or allied and/or coalition nations. (JP 1-02)

information. 1. Facts, data, or instructions in any medium or form. 2. The meaning that a human assigns to data by means of the known conventions used in their representation. (JP 1-02)

information requirements. In intelligence usage, those items of information regarding the adversary and other relevant aspects of the operational environment that need to be collected and processed in order to meet the intelligence requirements of a commander. (JP 1-02)

infrared imagery. That imagery produced as a result of sensing electromagnetic radiations emitted or reflected from a given target surface in the infrared position of the electromagnetic spectrum (approximately 0.72 to 1,000 microns). (JP 1-02)

intelligence. The product resulting from the collection, processing, integration, evaluation, analysis, and interpretation of available information concerning foreign nations, hostile or potentially hostile forces or elements, or areas of actual or potential operations. The term is also applied to the activity which results in the product and to the organizations engaged in such activity. (JP 2-0)

intelligence federation. A formal agreement in which a combatant command joint intelligence center receives preplanned intelligence support from other joint intelligence centers, Service intelligence organizations, Reserve organizations, and national agencies during crisis or contingency operations. (JP 2-01)

intelligence process. The process by which information is converted into intelligence and made available to users. The process consists of six interrelated intelligence operations: planning and direction, collection, processing and exploitation, analysis and production, dissemination and integration, and evaluation and feedback. (JP 1-02)

intelligence preparation of the battlespace. The analytical methodologies employed by the Services or joint force component commands to reduce uncertainties concerning the enemy, environment, time, and terrain. Intelligence preparation of the battlespace supports the individual operations of the joint force component commands. (JP 1-02)

intelligence preparation of the operational environment. The analytical process used by intelligence organizations to produce intelligence estimates and other intelligence products in support of the joint force commander's decision-making process. It is a continuous process that includes defining the operational environment; describing the impact of the operational environment; evaluating the adversary; and determining adversary courses of action. (JP 1-02)

intelligence requirement. 1. Any subject, general or specific, upon which there is a need for the collection of information, or the production of intelligence. 2. A requirement for intelligence to fill a gap in the command's knowledge or understanding of the operational environment or threat forces. (JP 1-02)

intelligence summary. A specific report providing a summary of items of intelligence at frequent intervals. (JP 1-02)

intelligence, surveillance, and reconnaissance. An activity that synchronizes and integrates the planning and operation of sensors, assets, and processing, exploitation, and dissemination systems in direct support of current and future operations. This is an integrated intelligence and operations function. (JP 1-02)

interoperability. 1. The ability to operate in synergy in the execution of assigned tasks. 2. The condition achieved among communications-electronics systems or items of communications-electronics equipment when information or services can be exchanged directly and satisfactorily between them and/or their users. The degree of interoperability should be defined when referring to specific cases. (JP 1-02)

interpretation. A part of the analysis and production phase in the intelligence process in which the significance of information is judged in relation to the current body of knowledge. See also intelligence process. (JP 1-02)

joint force. A general term applied to a force composed of significant elements, assigned or attached, of two or more Military Departments operating under a single joint force commander. (JP 1-02)

joint force air component commander. The commander within a unified command, subordinate unified command, or joint task force responsible to the establishing commander for making recommendations on the proper employment of assigned, attached, and/or made available for tasking air forces; planning and coordinating air operations; or accomplishing such operational missions as may be assigned. The joint force air component commander is given the authority necessary to accomplish missions and tasks assigned by the establishing commander.
(JP 1-02)

joint force commander. A general term applied to a combatant commander, subunified commander, or joint task force commander authorized to exercise combatant command (command authority) or operational control over a joint force. (JP 1-02)

joint task force. A joint force that is constituted and so designated by the Secretary of Defense, a combatant commander, a subunified commander, or an existing joint task force commander. (JP 1-02)

measurement and signature intelligence. Intelligence obtained by quantitative and qualitative analysis of data (metric, angle, spatial, wavelength, time dependence, modulation, plasma, and hydromagnetic) derived from specific technical sensors for the purpose of identifying any distinctive features associated with the emitter or sender, and to facilitate subsequent identification and/or measurement of the same. The detected feature may be either reflected or emitted. (JP 1-02)

mission assurance. Measures required to accomplish essential objectives of missions in a contested environment. Mission assurance entails prioritizing mission essential functions, mapping mission dependence on cyberspace, identifying vulnerabilities, and mitigating risk of known vulnerabilities. (AFDD 3-12)

monitoring. 1. The act of listening, carrying out surveillance on, and/or recording the emissions of one's own or allied forces for the purposes of maintaining and improving procedural standards and security, or for reference, as applicable. 2. The act of listening, carrying out surveillance on, and/or recording of enemy emissions for intelligence purposes. (JP 1-02)

national intelligence support team. A nationally sourced team composed of intelligence and communications experts from Defense Intelligence Agency, Central Intelligence Agency, National Geospatial-Intelligence Agency, National Security Agency, or other intelligence community agencies as required. (JP 1-02)

near-real time. Pertaining to the timeliness of data or information which has been delayed by the time required for electronic communication and automatic data processing. This implies that there are no significant delays. (JP 1-02)

open-source intelligence. Information of potential intelligence value that is available to the general public. (JP 1-02)

operational control. Command authority that may be exercised by commanders at any echelon at or below the level of combatant command. Operational control is inherent in combatant command (command authority) and may be delegated within the command. Operational control is the authority to perform those functions of command over subordinate forces involving organizing and employing commands and forces, assigning tasks, designating objectives, and giving authoritative direction necessary to accomplish the mission. Operational control includes authoritative direction over all aspects of military operations and joint training necessary to accomplish missions assigned to the command. Operational control should be exercised through the commanders of subordinate organizations. Normally this authority is exercised through subordinate joint force commanders and Service and/or functional component commanders. Operational control normally provides full authority to organize commands and forces and to employ those forces as the commander in operational control considers necessary to accomplish assigned missions; it does not, in and of itself, include authoritative direction for logistics or matters of administration, discipline, internal organization, or unit training. (JP 1-02)

operational environment. A composite of the conditions, circumstances, and influences that affect the employment of capabilities and bear on the decisions of the commander. (JP 1-02)

operational intelligence. Intelligence that is required for planning and conducting campaigns and major operations to accomplish strategic objectives within theaters or operational areas. (JP 1-02)

planning and direction. In intelligence usage, the determination of intelligence requirements, development of appropriate intelligence architecture, preparation of a collection plan, and issuance of orders and requests to information collection agencies. (JP 1-02)

priority intelligence requirements. An intelligence requirement, stated as a priority for intelligence support, that the commander and staff need to understand the adversary or the operational environment. (JP 1-02)

processing and exploitation. In intelligence usage, the conversion of collected information into forms suitable to the production of intelligence. (JP 1-02)

radar imagery. Imagery produced by recording radar waves reflected from a given target surface. (JP 1-02)

reachback. The process of obtaining products, services, and applications, or forces, or equipment, or material from organizations that are not forward deployed. (JP 1-02)

real time. Pertaining to the timeliness of data or information which has been delayed only by the time required for electronic communication. This implies that there are no noticeable delays. (JP 1-02)

reconnaissance. A mission undertaken to obtain, by visual observation or other detection methods, information about the activities and resources of an enemy or adversary, or to secure data concerning the meteorological, hydrographic, or geographic characteristics of a particular area. (JP 1-02)

request for information. 1. Any specific time-sensitive ad hoc requirement for intelligence information or products to support an ongoing crisis or operation not necessarily related to standing requirements or scheduled intelligence production. A request for information can be initiated to respond to operational requirements and will be validated in accordance with the combatant command's procedures. 2. The National Security Agency/Central Security Service uses this term to state ad hoc signals intelligence requirements. (JP 1-02)

scientific and technical intelligence. The product resulting from the collection, evaluation, analysis, and interpretation of foreign scientific and technical information that covers: a. foreign developments in basic and applied research and in applied engineering techniques; and b. scientific and technical characteristics, capabilities, and limitations of all foreign military systems, weapons, weapon systems, and materiel; the research and development related thereto; and the production methods employed for their manufacture. (JP 1-02)

sensor. A device that responds to a physical stimulus (as heat, light, sound, pressure, magnetism, or a particular motion) and transmits a resulting impulse (as for measurement or operating a control).

SIGINT operational tasking authority. A military commander's authority to operationally direct and levy signals intelligence (SIGINT) requirements on designated SIGINT resources; includes authority to deploy and redeploy all or part of the SIGINT resources for which SIGINT operational tasking authority has been delegated. (JP 1-02)

signals intelligence. 1. A category of intelligence comprising either individually or in combination all communications intelligence, electronic intelligence, and foreign instrumentation signals intelligence, however transmitted. 2. Intelligence derived from communications, electronic, and foreign instrumentation signals. (JP 1-02)

special operations. Operations conducted in hostile, denied, or politically sensitive environments to achieve military, diplomatic, informational, and/or economic objectives employing military capabilities for which there is no broad conventional force requirement. These operations often require covert, clandestine, or low visibility capabilities. Special operations are applicable across the range of military operations. They can be conducted independently or in conjunction with operations of conventional forces or other government agencies and may include operations through, with, or by indigenous or surrogate forces. Special operations differ from conventional operations in degree of physical and political risk, operational techniques, mode of employment, independence from friendly support, and dependence on detailed operational intelligence and indigenous assets. (JP 1-02)

surveillance. The systematic observation of aerospace, surface, or subsurface areas, places, persons, or things, by visual, aural, electronic, photographic, or other means. (JP 1-02)

tactical control. Command authority over assigned or attached forces or commands, or military capability or forces made available for tasking, that is limited to the detailed direction and control of movements or maneuvers within the operational area necessary to accomplish missions or tasks assigned. Tactical control is inherent in operational control. Tactical control may be delegated to, and exercised at any level at or below the level of combatant command. Tactical control provides sufficient authority for controlling and directing the application of force or tactical use of combat support assets within the assigned mission or task. (JP 1-02)

target. 1. An entity or object considered for possible engagement or other action. 2. In intelligence usage, a country, area, installation, agency, or person against which intelligence operations are directed. 3. An area designated and numbered for future firing. 4. In gunfire support usage, an impact burst that hits the target. (JP 1-02)

targeting. The process of selecting and prioritizing targets and matching the appropriate response to them, considering operational requirements and capabilities. (JP 1-02)

technical intelligence. Intelligence derived from the collection, processing, analysis, and exploitation of data and information pertaining to foreign equipment and materiel for the purposes of preventing technological surprise, assessing foreign scientific and technical capabilities, and developing countermeasures designed to neutralize an adversary's technological advantages. (JP 1-02)

validation. 1. A process associated with the collection and production of intelligence that confirms that an intelligence collection or production requirement is sufficiently important to justify the dedication of intelligence resources, does not duplicate an existing requirement, and has not been previously satisfied. 2. A part of target development that ensures all vetted targets meet the objectives and criteria outlined in the commander's guidance and ensures compliance with the law of armed conflict and rules of engagement.   3. In computer modeling and simulation, the process of determining the degree to which a model or simulation is an accurate representation of the real world from the perspective of the intended uses of the model or simulation.   4. Execution procedure used by combatant command components, supporting combatant commanders, and providing organizations to confirm to the supported commander and United States Transportation Command that all the information records in a time-phased force and deployment data not only are error free for automation purposes, but also accurately reflect the current status, attributes, and availability of units and requirements. (JP 1-02)